IMPACT

IMPACT

Assessment, Treatment, and Prevention of Sexual Misconduct: Case Studies in Sexual Abuse

Janet Nekooasl-Smith, M.Ed.

iUniverse, Inc.

New York Lincoln Shanghai

IMPACT
Assessment, Treatment, and Prevention of Sexual Misconduct: Case Studies in Sexual Abuse

iUniverse books may be ordered through booksellers or by contacting:

iUniverse
2021 Pine Lake Road, Suite 100
Lincoln, NE 68512
www.iuniverse.com
1-800-Authors (1-800-288-4677)

ISBN-13: 978-0-595-34804-6 (pbk)
ISBN-13: 978-0-595-79537-6 (ebk)
ISBN-10: 0-595-34804-1 (pbk)
ISBN-10: 0-595-79537-4 (ebk)

Printed in the United States of America

Contents

Acknowledgments

I want to thank Dr. Eliana Gil for allowing me to consult with her on a regular basis and to benefit from her insight, knowledge, and professionalism. In many cases, she helped me understand dynamics that were happening before my eyes that I had missed. I admire her abilities in working with puppet interviews, sand-tray therapy, and art therapy. I admire most her skill at verbalizing ongoing dynamics, whether involving individual, family, or group treatment.

I thank Raymond Navarro, my colleague, for beginning the SORT Program with me (Sex Offender Relapse Prevention Treatment). I have benefited from his experience with treating sex offenders, and facilitating sex offender group treatment with him has been a pleasure.

I also thank Dr. William Tyson for his expertise and consultation on treating sex offenders. I have benefited greatly from his knowledge, understanding, and experience with treating sex offenders.

Introduction

When I began graduate school, I considered becoming a guidance counselor. I had previous experience teaching and coaching. The first class I enrolled in was Introduction to Counseling. One of the professor's requirements was for each student "to find twenty-five sources on something that interests you." I decided to find sources on sexual abuse because I did not know much about the issue at that time, and I desired a better understanding. Since then I have not stopped addressing the issue of sexual victimization, and to this day I still use some of those articles I found to help victims of sexual assault.

After graduation, I became the Director of Victim Services at a rape crisis center for approximately three years before entering private practice as a Licensed Professional Counselor for the past eleven years. My experience of providing services to victims in their hospital rooms while working at the rape crisis center provided me with a wealth of information and knowledge. Many rape crisis centers use volunteers to attend to victim needs. I have trained many volunteers on how to be there for a victim during this traumatic time in her or his life and found it to be emotionally rewarding. During this time as Director of Victim Services, I also learned a great deal about how the legal system works regarding victims. Once in private practice, I began working with families with sexual abusers. I began both educating myself about sex offenders and attending training in the treatment of sex offenders. I also began providing group treatment for sex offenders in three counties. I continue to provide group treatment for both survivors and offenders and to facilitate reunification with sex offenders when appropriate. Over the course of these eleven years, I have also treated individuals, couples, adolescents, and children who have struggled with the following issues: depression, anxiety, trauma, marital problems, parenting, grief, divorce, and behavioral problems.

Now I am publishing some practical guidelines that can help prevent sexual abuse. I am writing this book with the hope that many individuals will be able to benefit from these guidelines and identify ways to keep children safe. This book is unique in that it addresses the complex areas of sexual violations rather than focusing on one of the specific populations that need treatment: victims, offenders, or spouses. Sexual abuse is not a one-population issue, nor is it a gender problem. Even though more males are convicted of sexual misconduct, more and more females are being convicted.

Adults have done a less-than-adequate job of protecting children. Many children who have been sexually abused had one or both parents who were sexually abused themselves. However, these parents have usually not addressed their own victimization until one or both are charged with a crime or when someone else is charged with a crime against their child. Even then, the adults generally want help for their child while ignoring their own need for treatment. Today it is easier to locate and identify present sex offenders as evidenced by those who are required to register. Conversely, the sex offenders out there who have never been convicted and are currently offending are the most dangerous factor and the greatest cause for concern. Nevertheless, if adults will utilize the information given in this book, begin to recognize risk behaviors, challenge their old beliefs, and put their new beliefs into practice, then children can be safer.

Chapter 1 identifies the stages that victims of sexual assault can pass through during the life span and includes a case example.

Chapter 2 discusses some factors that influence the effects on victims and gives an accurate account of the grooming behaviors of sex offenders.

Chapter 3 demonstrates ways in which offenders give themselves permission to commit sexual offenses, as well as ways that victims make sense of what happened to them; I then describe how parents and other caretakers cope with the issues of sexual victimization.

Chapter 4 is one of the most intriguing chapters because it deals with the similarities between victims and offenders, which is an issue that few members of society consider—especially victims. Many victims are unaware of how their offender's thinking affects their own thinking and creates similarities between the two.

Chapter 5 explores the treatment of all those involved and the important stages of coping with having been a survivor, an offender, or a significant other.

Chapter 6 presents case examples of the ways that sex offenses are committed and offers changes individuals can make to ensure that children are safe.

Chapter 7 summarizes the ways sexual victimization impacts individuals.

This book is titled *Impact* because once someone has been sexually offended, the impact remains for years. Victims, offenders, and significant others are forced to deal with the after effects for the rest of their lives. Professionals in the field today are engaging in relevant discussions about harm reduction. From the following chapters, you will be able to gain a fuller picture of the impact of sexual violations. You will be challenged to examine your current attitudes and beliefs about offenders, survivors, and significant others. In doing so, you will be able to make more informed decisions about protecting children. I have changed the names in the cases I've cited to protect these individuals' privacy. In addition, although neither victims nor offenders are gender specific and can be male or female, I have referred to victims in the female gender and offenders in the male gender for simplicity.

1

The Impact of Sexual Violations over the Life Span

One of the saddest sexual assault cases I ever worked with involved Joe, a thirty-nine-year-old male who went into therapy because he suffered from depression and thoughts of suicide. He also had other severe medical problems, including diabetic neuropathy, and he was attempting to receive disability benefits. I worked with Joe for thirteen sessions over a six-month period. He was turned down for disability several times according to him and his spouse because of his age. This patient, who used to be a bouncer in a nightclub and a lover of the outdoors in Alaska, could barely walk in his present condition and used a cane for ambulation. Due to Joe's poor health, he had difficulty discussing emotional concerns.

After we worked through his thoughts of suicide, he wanted to discuss the sexual abuse he had survived. He was highly medicated and on several occasions slept through the session. He mostly wanted to discuss having been sexually abused when he was a child. He had never before talked about his own victimization. He had been sexually abused by adult males and had a lot of shame about what had happened to him. He was dyslexic and thus could not read any material about sexual abuse. I understood how difficult it would be for him to resolve sexual abuse issues because of his medicated state and learning disability, and I supported him as much as I could. He would tell me I was helping him by encouraging him to verbally express what he had been holding in for years regarding his sexual abuse. We discussed how many people who are abused by someone of the same sex tend to confuse their abuse with homosexuality. They may struggle with their sexuality from time to time all throughout their lives. I agreed with Joe that talking about these past experiences was helpful; however, I knew that, given his medical conditions, he might not have the time to completely resolve what had happened to him, and, for that reason I did not feel especially helpful at the time. I kept thinking to myself, "This man is going to die," and I was genuinely concerned he might die in my office. He did indeed die from complications of diabetes after six months of therapy. His wife called several months after his death to inform me that he had received his disability benefits.

What was the impact of the sexual assault on this man's life? It was clearly significant in that he had attempted to talk about it during his final days. He never expressed that he knew he was dying, but I believe he knew. For many, the impact of sexual assault can be so long lasting that, even when people are dying, they feel the need to resolve what happened to them. Joe's courage in trying, during his dying days, to resolve having been sexually assaulted as a child is admirable.

Most people who have been sexually violated go through phases of processing their own victimization. If the victims were children at the time of the assault—provided that the sexual violations were reported and adjudicated—they are likely to have been referred for therapy. Developmentally, these children can only participate in limited therapy and may need to return to therapy later on in life. The need for this later therapy may arise because the survivors are still suffering distress from the sexual violations, or because they want to examine, as adults, how the sexual violations might still be affecting them. In some cases, adult victims still view their sexual violations from a childlike perspective.

As children develop and age, they go through phases of thinking about what happened to them. During a conference given by Jan Hindman, past president of the Association for the Treatment of Sexual Abusers, she identified four stages through which a victim of sexual assault might pass. (Hindman gave permission to the audience members to refer to these phases to help victims in therapy or in publication.) Adult victims feel reassured when they read the stages and often find that they have passed through one or more of them.

The first phase is the *unaware* phase. Children lack the cognitive ability to understand what is being done to them. They respond in fear to the sex offenders (authority figures) who are sexually violating them, possibly threatening them and encouraging secrecy about the act. They also respond in fear because of their own lack of understanding or they experience shock about what is being done to them. At this stage, children and many teens do not understand that they cannot legally consent to sexual contact, and sex offenders use this lack of understanding to manipulate, force, or otherwise coerce victims into such contact.

In the next stage, the *unfortunate* phase, children re-examine what was done to them. This occurs—on some level—throughout the life span. Children in this stage look backward and begin to frequently experience overwhelming shame, guilt, humiliation, or embarrassment. They often blame themselves by using thinking errors. As children develop sexually, they question their behavior during the sexual offense. What they do not understand at a young age is that the body automatically responds to sexual touching, and there is no control over the response to sexual stimulation, just as there is no control over the tears one sheds when one peels an onion. Thus said, their bodies responded and they are not responsible, and the sexual offenses were not their fault.

The third stage is the *uncomfortable* phase. Once the survivors experience shame, humiliation, guilt, or embarrassment, they generally exhibit anger, rage, or defiance. There appears to be an overwhelming "badness" in survivors in this phase of sexual development. They may engage in negative behavior, such as sexual promiscuity, oppositional/defiant behavior, or juvenile delinquency stemming from a belief that they are "bad," and they therefore attempt to match their behavior to that belief.

The last stage is the *unresolved* phase. The children have become adults and often experience anxiety, depression, or low self-esteem. They begin to examine the impact of having been sexually violated. They start to remember correctly (not blaming themselves), and they embark on the process of holding the sexual offenders accountable for their behavior. They gradually let go of the self-blame, shame, humiliation, guilt, or embarrassment and recognize their innocence as children. This is the stage in which healing begins. The sense of badness is placed on the offenders where it rightfully belongs, and as adults, the victims evolve from survivors to people who view themselves as deserving of respect and dignity.

Survivors generally reach this phase in a therapeutic setting. People who were sexually violated as adults will also experience some aspects of these stages. They generally go through the last three stages. They do not tend to experience the unaware stage—except in the case of an adult who was drugged or is mentally challenged (for whom the mental capacity to understand what is being done to them is unavailable).

Victims want to know why they were sexually offended. Their quest is to make sense of what happened to them. However, I tell victims that directly asking sex offenders why is not as significant as asking how they gave themselves permission to sexually offend. Asking sex offenders why they sexually offended sets up a scenario in which the offenders will lie to the survivors. Asking people why they did something puts them on the defense. Sex offenders are defensive before any questions are asked, and asking them why causes them to fabricate inadequate answers that do not benefit the survivors, especially if the sex offenders are untreated. Even treated offenders give answers in which they fail to take full responsibility for their actions. When survivors ask why, they are seeking an admission of guilt, an apology, and an acknowledgment of harm. It is rare that survivors get an admission of guilt regarding sexually inappropriate behavior, an apology, or an acknowledgment of harm from offenders. Therefore, the simple answer to why they sexually offended is because they wanted to, they could, and they did.

When treating sex offenders, the focus is not on why they sexually offended, but on how they did so. The more important question is how the offenders planned their actions and manipulated, forced, or coerced others in order to violate them sexually. If sex offenders know how they offended, they can know what to look for to prevent their selves from doing the same thing again. A main concern of survivors is to ensure that the offender does not re-offend. Research by Karl Hanson supports the idea that the risk of repeat offenses decreases with successful completion of treatment; however, even with treatment, the risk of a repeat offense is ever present (Hanson, Bussiere, and Bussiere, 1998).

Even though the effects of sexual violations over the life span cannot be fully explained by the four phases, all those who have been sexually violated can choose to work through the impact. Ultimately, they can explore the impact on their own lives and decide for themselves whether they will remain victims of sexual violation or heal and move on to becoming survivors. Survivors want their loved ones (spouses, family members, friends, and so on) to understand their experiences and cope with their moods, which may be related to the sexual violations. Survivors often expect healing to come from external sources, such as an apology from the offender or understanding from others, but healing is an internal process that takes much emotional effort on the survivor's part.

2

Factors Influencing Impact: Age, Emotional Stability, Support System, Duration

The impact of sexual assault is subjective, and no one—including profession-als—can accurately identify all the ways in which survivors are affected. Some factors that can influence the impact of sexual violations include the survivor's age at the time of the violation, emotional stability, a support system, and the duration of the sexual assault.

Age

The age of the survivor is as significant as the survivor's perception of age at the time of the assault. Some survivors say that they were young, and the sex-ual assault did not affect them much, whereas others are devastated no matter what their age was. Regardless of their age at the time of the violation, survi-vors will cope with the impact on various levels throughout their lives.

I had a client in therapy in her mid-forties—I'll call her Sue—who had been laid off from her management position with one of the airlines after the September 11, 2001, terrorist attack on the World Trade Center. Sue informed me up front that she did not like therapists. She had previously been in therapy with her husband and his therapist for marital difficulties. I began to explore her history with her. She had been kidnapped and sexually assaulted around age five; she had also been raped at age fifteen, and her first sexual experience was by a twenty-one-year-old man when she was thirteen. Having sexual contact with a minor is a sex crime in many states. In Sue's case, she had not told anyone that the kidnapper had sexually assaulted her—not the police or her mother, who were waiting at home when the kidnapper released her near her house. The kidnapper was never found. To this day, Sue has not told anyone outside therapy that she was sexually assaulted then; even her husband has no idea.

Sue's daughter Holly had been sexually abused by an eighty-year-old neighbor when she was about five years old. Sue was burdened with guilt about Holly's sexual abuse. No charges had ever been filed, and Holly could press charges against her offender if the man were still living because there is no statute of limitations on sex crimes in her state. Holly, now fifteen years old, was currently involved with a nineteen-year-old military man. Sue saw nothing wrong with this relationship; even though it was certainly a risky situ-ation for both the man and Holly, neither of them viewed it as such. As a therapist, I had to be extremely careful of what I said to Sue about this. I knew that if I said anything Sue might misconstrue, she would voluntarily discon-tinue therapy. I cringed at the thought of the sex offenders I had treated in the age range of eighteen to twenty years who had sexually assaulted girls in the thirteen- to fifteen-year-old age range. Sue was living vicariously through her daughter, thinking that Holly was sexually sophisticated and wishing that she had been as sexually sophisticated as her daughter. Sue had never gone to therapy to explore the impact of the sexual assaults on her own life. She neither considered her first nominally voluntary sexual experience a sexual violation—when it technically was—nor did she recognize that her decision-making ability had been impaired because of her own sexual victimizations. As she ages, it remains to be seen when and if she will begin the task of exploring the impact of sexual assault on her own life. She was invited to participate in a survivors group but refused; she had only come to therapy for anxiety over the loss of her job.

When mothers have young daughters who have been sexually violated, they often believe their children will not remember the sexual abuse and it will never bother them again. That is possible; however, it is highly likely that a memory of sexual assault could be triggered by something, such as a sound, smell, movie, person, or something else at some point in their lives. In addition, survivors may have a body memory but no memory of the actual assault. A body memory is when one has an odd feeling when being touched but she cannot connect the memory with the actual life experience. Mothers are generally uncomfortable discussing their daughters' sexual assault with them. In Sue's case, she and I discussed her talking with Holly about the sexual abuse she had survived. Sue thought Holly did not remember the abuse. Holly did remember the abuse and told her mother that it did not bother her. However, Holly had not had enough life experience to know how the sexual abuse might eventually impact her. She was still a teenager and not yet sexually active. Even though she was dating a nineteen-year-old male, both alleged they were not having a sexual relationship. Once she becomes sexually active, the effects of the sexual abuse could be triggered along with feelings about the sexual assault. Because this mother was sexually assaulted at an early age and had not worked through any of her sexual assault experiences or that of her daughter, it is difficult for her to define the impact of her own sexual victimization. To demonstrate to Sue how sly and manipulative sex offenders are, I encouraged her to read the following, in which Michael O'Connell describes how sex offenders "groom" their victims, their victim's family, and the environment.

Material resources are used in two basic ways: to aid the offender in preparing to commit his crime, and to set up a victim to be assaulted. One offender may use his vehicle to cruise, searching for likely victims or locations, whereas another may use the vehicle as an enticement, trading a driving lesson for sexual favors. Alcohol or other mood-altering substances may be consumed to reduce inhibitions or to establish a defense ("I was too drunk; I didn't know what I was doing"). They may also be used as a trap for victims, either to lure them into situations where offending can occur or to provide leverage to keep the victims silent ("If your mother knew you were smoking pot, she'd kill you. If you tell her about what we did I will tell her you started it when you were on drugs.")

Grooming may be the most important of all antecedent behaviors to understand. Grooming is broadly defined as any activity that desensitizes the victim or significant others for the purpose of enabling a sexual offense to occur. Victims, the family, neighbors, acquaintances, and the community may all be groomed.

There are many types of grooming, which include physical, psychological, and environmental grooming. *Physical grooming* begins with behavior that children and adults would consider appropriate. This physical contact becomes grooming behavior when it is used to accustom a victim to touching that can lead to sexual involvement. For example, the offender may use back rubs to desensitize the victim to more and more intrusive physical contact. A child sitting on an adult's lap is being groomed when the adult keeps the child there despite having an erection. Initially, the adult makes no comment or movement. If the child seems not to notice, the adult may joke about the erection. If a child shows curiosity, the adult may offer to show the child his penis. This may lead to the adult asking to see the child's genitals or allowing the adult to touch the child. All of this is presented as a normal, nonthreatening activity.

Grooming falls in a spectrum from subtle to obvious to overt. By gaining the victim's acceptance through normal physical contact, the offender begins to break down the victim's acceptance through normal physical contact, the offender begins to break down the victim's resistance. The offender induces confusion in the victim when behavior that seemed appropriate at first becomes less appropriate. Grooming activities provide a reach-and-retreat behavioral repertoire during which the offender can test a victim's level of resistance, resolve, and vulnerability. The reach-and-retreat approach also provides a ready escape or excuse from accusations if confronted by either the child or others.

Psychological grooming may occur in a variety of ways, including the promise of material items or...special privileges. Skillful manipulation can create an indebtedness, which the offender can later use. For example, he may allow a child to stay up past regular bedtime and promise not to tell the child's mother. This works especially well when the child knows this is against the mother's wishes. It becomes even more effective when the offender is able to convince the child that, if the secret is revealed, the child will be punished rather than the offender who gave permission. Manipulations of this kind create compacts between the offender and the victim and barriers between the child and the nonoffending caretaker. When offending finally begins, the child fears revealing the problem because it will lead to disclosing all of the child's other bad behaviors.

An offender may also create states of fear and uncertainty in the victim's mind. For example, the offender might read a newspaper article about another sex offender and say, "That poor man was treated unfairly, and now a cruel judge is sending him to prison for the rest of his life, just for playing with children." The offender can later use this information to manipulate the victim into agreeing not to disclose the offense. Offenders can issue covert threats with statements such as (a) "Children who do not obey their parents should be beaten," (b) "Adults know better than children what's right," or (C) "Children should not ask questions, but only do as they are told."

Some victims are especially vulnerable by virtue of their isolation, prior abuse, or other factors. The offender may present a grooming style that is immediately rewarding and pleasing to these children. He may spend special time playing, traveling, providing entertainment, or just listening and talking with a child who feels neglected. The offender may listen to the child's problems and give advice. Then, gradually, the offender may introduce his own problems, giving the child a sense of importance and wisdom by eliciting the child's advice. Grooming escalates when the offender begins to talk about problems between himself and the child's mother. He subtly or directly introduces the idea that the child can give comfort, emotional support, and love to the offender that the mother cannot or will not give because she has her own problems. The offender lays the groundwork for this kind of bond to lead to sexual exploitation later on. The effect is to create a sense that the offender and the child really understand one another. Flattery heightens the child's interest at this stage. Dwelling on the mother's problems increases the likelihood that grooming will proceed with the potential resistance of the child decreased.

Psychological grooming can make the trauma to the victim severe. The child may believe the deceits laid out by the offender, and that belief is reinforced by the memory of shared warmth and tenderness. The child's sense of importance and maturity is increased. All of these, as well as the child's sense of self-esteem and adequacy, are undermined upon disclosing the offense. Guilt, self-doubt, pain, anger, and despair are natural consequences to a child-victim of such carefully plotted grooming behavior.

An offender may also *groom other persons* to increase his access to potential victims. He may offer to do special tasks, projects, or activities for a child's mother that create the opportunity for her to be away from the home and victim. By working long hours himself, the offender may claim that the mother should do more financially and point out the swing-swift waitress job in a city miles away. The mother may also be groomed in a negative sense by the offender constantly criticizing her, creating a desire in her to simply get away from the home. This emotional climate makes the prospects of a swing-shift or graveyard job more inviting to the mother. Without realizing it, she has been steered in a direction away from the home. The offender is now in a better position to sexually abuse the child.

Finally, *environmental grooming* occurs when the offender grooms persons outside the victim's home to increase his access to children. For example, an offender may work with children through schools or community youth groups and perform many worthwhile services. But he may also take advantage of this position and use it to arrange times to be alone with potential victims. By establishing an image of a benefactor to the community, he engenders a special trust. As a result, the mere suggestion by anyone that this person may have abused a child is often met with disbelief. The community may be inclined to side with the offender, proclaiming the impossibility of the charges because of the certainty that the offender "is just a caring individual who loves children." Once official charges have been made, those who have regular contact with and sometimes rely on the accused in various ways must then begin to grapple with what his loss will mean if he is convicted. The community may lose his committee work and his organizational or other valuable abilities. The offender often has spent much time being visible in activities that lessened the workload of those around him. This reinforces the willingness of others to put children under his care and makes the community disinclined to believe that he could do anything wrong.

In one case, a schoolteacher was convicted of sexually abusing two female students. During the pre-sentence investigation, the probation officer received no less than 50 separate letters from supporters of the teacher. Every letter contained examples of contributions the teacher had made to the school. Other teachers described how he had made their jobs easier because of his willingness to handle less desirable extracurricular tasks. The majority of the letters referred to the victims as having bad reputations and claimed that they were at least partially to blame. Only 2 of the 50 letters showed any understanding of the basic facts of the case, which clearly indicated that the teacher had used force in his offenses. This teacher had made extensive efforts to groom an entire educational community, including students, parents, staff, and administrators.

A candid exploration and discussion of grooming behaviors by the evaluator is essential in cutting through the façade that sex offenders often construct. This facade, as long as it is permitted to stand, prevents the criminal justice system from dealing with this offender in the same objective manner in which it treats other less skillful and manipulative offenders. Allowing the façade to remain also undermines the belief in the need for effective community surveillance and supervision. Disclosure of the grooming behavior helps to penetrate the facade and to establish the appropriate structure necessary to help prevent re-offense.

A clear discussion of grooming also helps victims and other family members see how skillfully they were manipulated and how carefully structured the offender's efforts were to break down their will and sense of self-protection. This process can be instrumental in helping victims and family members break through their confusion and deal more constructively with their feelings about the offense.

Failing to break down this façade would be counterproductive to the offender and his therapy. It would allow the offender to persist in his belief that he has a host of redeeming characteristics, which are, in reality, simply a solid base for his own deviancy. The therapist who allows these virtues to persist unchallenged is not likely to recognize or challenge the true extent of the offender's deviant system. By maintaining the false image, the offender is likely to forget the psychological trauma inflicted on the victim and the toll his behavior has taken on the community as a whole. If the façade persists, the offender will not be able to examine the darker, manipulative aspects of his good deeds to see how they served as a safe base from which to initiate molesting behaviors. Understanding offender manipulation in all its forms helps explain the extent of an offender's deviancy. It also provides a basis for supervision and surveillance of an offender who is allowed to remain in the community. A thorough evaluation should consider and provide assistance to those persons responsible for community supervision by carefully analyzing these antecedent behaviors.

(Reprinted with permission from *Working with Sex Offenders*, Sage Publications, Inc., 1990)

Survivors are frequently too busy blaming themselves to see how they or other family members were groomed. After reading the article, Sue stated that she was angry with me. Her anger was displaced because she did not want to deal with her own sexual abuse history. For Sue, the impact of her sexual abuse caused her to avoid confronting her emotional pain surrounding the sexual assaults that had been a part of her life.

Some survivors become emotionally stuck at the age they were when they were sexually violated. They have difficulty in their relationships, marriages, parenting, and other areas of their lives because they are operating as if they were much younger. As a result, they are not sufficiently mature to deal with the everyday decisions and events in their adult reality. For example, I worked with an adult who still behaved in the same ways she did when she was fifteen. At that age, an adult male had sexually violated her, impregnated her, and then abandoned her. She gave the child up for adoption. Two failed marriages later, she entered therapy with me because of her depression. It took three years before she could discuss this painful series of events in her life. She attended about eight sessions the first year, four sessions the second year, and approximately eight sessions the third year before she could address how her experience at fifteen had kept her stuck in her life. In essence, these survivors need to go through a period of maturation. Other survivors who have had more of their basic needs met and a strong support system after the sexual violation do not have this tendency to get emotionally stuck.

Emotional Stability

Sexual assault generally affects survivors' emotional stability to some degree. Many survivors do not have a strong support system upon disclosure of a sexual assault. Even for those who do have a strong support system, the emotional consequences of a sexual assault disclosure can be emotionally taxing. For minors, if the offender is a family member, either the offender or the survivor is removed from the home—either of which is devastating to the survivor. For some survivors, this consequence is worse than the sexual assault. That does not mean they wanted the sexual assault, but that they want their family to be together without any sexually inappropriate behavior. In many cases, the survivors' emotional stability is questioned, or the survivors are considered emotionally unstable by the mother, the police, or especially the offender. Defense attorneys may portray survivors as unstable. Some offenders know their victims were admitted to a psychiatric ward and present them as the problem rather than focusing on their own deviant behavior. Offenders fail or otherwise refuse to consider the fact that the victims may have been admitted for hospitalization because of the offenders' behavior—until confronted with this idea when they are in treatment.

No matter the age when survivors were assaulted, they know their emotional stability has been scrutinized, and they often question their own emotional state or sanity. An example is a case I worked with before it was adjudicated. The stepfather, Frank, had allegedly been sexually inappropriate with his stepdaughter, Brittany, on three separate occasions. Both of the parents reported that they had been sexually abused as children, though neither had sought therapy to deal with their own victimization issues. They had attempted to work out Frank's behavior with his stepdaughter through a pastor without involving the legal system, and they were angry with the pastor for reporting Frank and for the resulting involvement of child protective services.

Frank was removed from the home, a guilt-producing experience for the survivor. All three family members were questioning the victim's emotional stability. Brittany (the victim), Diane (her mother), and Frank (the stepfather and offender) all focused on when Brittany had tried to convince her middle school class the previous year that she was dracula reincarnated. Even though Diane was trying to be supportive by telling Brittany that Frank's behavior was not her fault, the implication of the focus on the dracula incident was that Brittany was lying about the alleged sexually inappropriate behavior. The information about the dracula incident was defocusing and a way for Diane and Frank to avoid taking responsibility, Frank for any sexual misconduct and Diane for not protecting her daughter. He was convicted of sexual misconduct and was ordered by the court to get treatment.

When Brittany remembers and examines her sexual victimization as an adult, how will she see herself emotionally? Can she identify the impact of sexual assault at the present time? How will she consider herself to have been impacted when she is an adult?

As noted earlier, the impact of sexual assault changes throughout the life span, in part because victims' cognitive abilities change. Survivors are generally able to think more accurately about the sexual assault as they age. Yet one result of sexual assault is that survivors continue to view the sexual assault from a child's perspective. The mind wants things to change—for the sexual assault never to have occurred; however, facts cannot change, only how survivors view the facts can change. Many survivors of sexual assault become emotionally weaker at some point in their lives. This could occur when they are first sexually assaulted, or it could be years later when they are trying to work through the assault.

One survivor I worked with eventually had a breakdown in her mid-thirties and was hospitalized. When Judy and her husband, Dave, both then in their fifties, decided to go into therapy with me because of marital issues, they had been to three other therapists, but none of them had discussed Judy's sexual assault history. When Judy was eight years old, a male neighbor who was a deacon in the church began exposing himself to her and fondling her. He would gain access to her when she would go to his house to play with his daughter. He would send his daughter to the store and make Judy stay at the house with him. Judy never told anyone. At age twenty, she and Dave—who was at that time her fiancée—were making out in the car while parked at the airport, as many couples in the area did. Four black men appeared, locked Dave in the trunk, and each of the four raped her while holding a gun to her head. One comment she remembered them saying to her was, "what is your daddy going to say when you have a black baby?"

Which one of these sexual assaults impacted her more? Judy stated that she had more difficulty with the sexual assault that took place when she was a young child than the rapes when she was an adult. Judy and Dave had marital problems for most of their thirty-plus years of marriage. Judy linked a smile that the deacon had exhibited with a smile Dave had, but she never talked about this during any of her previous therapy sessions. She stated that she felt her earlier therapists were afraid to discuss the issue. The three of us talked about it, and eventually Dave stated that he knew what smile she was talking about. Even though Judy noted that the childhood sexual assault affected her more, it could be that she was still avoiding dealing with the rapes. Judy had frequent nightmares, and she would wake up screaming, waking Dave. Before they could complete their therapy work together as a couple, Dave was diagnosed with lung cancer and told me they no longer needed my services because they had discovered the more important things in life.

The most remarkable adult survivor I have worked with was Katrina. I had six sessions with her. She was thirty-four when she began therapy. Katrina had an emotional breakdown as a result of her father—who was a minister—having sexually abused her when she was twelve. Her emotional breakdown came when she went to confront her father when she was age forty, and he pulled a gun on her and her husband. She had not received therapy prior to this time, and it is not recommended that survivors confront offenders without having had therapy. Even with therapy, the risk of confrontation is re-victimization, which is what happened to Katrina. Her father, by pulling a gun on her, had victimized her all over again. It was an assault, although Katrina did not press any charges. His denial of any sexual misconduct was also re-victimizing. Her mother not believing her was also re-victimizing. After the confrontation, she eventually decided not to have any contact with her family.

Katrina was exceptionally good at verbalizing what had happened to her, not blaming herself, holding the offender responsible, and moving on with her life. She did all the homework assignments I gave her, which included reading several articles and books. She was able to discuss what her father had done to her openly, without shame and guilt, and to recognize that her body had responded sexually as any human body would, regardless of the circumstances. As she worked through the homework assignments I gave her, she remembered other times that she had been sexually assaulted. She remembered her sister's husband sexually abusing her when she was a minor. She had never met another person who she knew had been sexually assaulted, so I had a session with Katrina and Judy. Judy was amazed at Katrina's emotional stability and ability to verbalize what had happened to her. She was vibrant, confident, and full of life—qualities survivors admire. Many survivors remain in therapy for longer periods of time and do not reach that joy of life that Katrina had.

Support System

All too frequently, neither the survivor nor the sex offender has an adequate support system. Survivors are frequently blamed in some way for having been sexually violated. This is a contributing factor to delayed disclosure, no matter the age of the victim. The survivors seem to intuitively know that they will be blamed. Adolescent survivors are targeted by their mothers, by the sex offenders, and by the legal system as having more of a motive to lie than younger survivors. Society has a preconceived idea that some adolescents do not like their stepfathers, fathers, or whomever they accuse, and therefore make up a lie to get what they want. That is true in some cases, but it is rare. Mothers have a motive not to believe their adolescent children, because their own economic security is disrupted once children disclose sexual violations when the offenders are the fathers or stepfathers.

What often happens now is that the offenders are made to leave the home rather than the children being removed, which used to be standard protocol. The previous procedures were used because the workers thought removing the children was in the best interest of the child. Over time, workers began to recognize this made the children feel as if they had done something wrong and increased the victims' feelings of being blamed, when it was of course the offenders who had done wrong. Child protective services often become involved, which the parents resent and resist, and then the parents tend to blame the child or someone else for the outside involvement. The parents have a tendency to blame the people who made the report to child protective services, such as family members or friends. In many cases, it is the mandated reporter who gets blamed: the mental health counselor, school counselor, pastors, or any one who is required to report a suspected sexual offense. Some blame is not laid in a direct manner. It is done with statements that have underlying implications, like the bringing up of the dracula event described earlier. When survivors hear parents saying, "She convinced the whole school she was dracula," or "She is a pathological liar," they shut down, go into a kind of shock, and cannot or will not respond. In relation to the dracula statement, the implication was that the daughter was a good liar, and that she was also lying about her stepfather having touched her in a sexual manner. By contrast, the younger the children are, the more likely they are to both be believed and have a stronger support system.

I worked with a mother, whom I'll call Joanne, who initially appeared to be a strong supporter. She admitted she blamed her child, had not initially believed her child, and she had to go back and apologize to her child. Her husband John had sexually offended her daughter (his stepdaughter) who was thirteen years old at the time. They also shared two biological daughters aged two and eleven years. Joanne was a mother who began asking herself some hard questions. Without any prodding from the therapist, Joanne was asking herself such questions as: Why didn't I see the signs? What kind of mother am I if I reunite with him? Are my other children at risk if I reunite? What will people think of me if I reunite with him?

These are valid questions. Meanwhile, John was only focused on when he could go back home, because he was in the initial stages of treatment and could not identify risky situations. John was able to work out through the courts that he would be allowed to return home at the discretion of the treatment providers. In his group treatment, it was pointed out to him that returning home prematurely was a high-risk situation for both him and his children. His victim, his stepdaughter, was already being re-victimized by child protective services. The caseworker told the victim, "You had better be glad I got John out of the home, otherwise you would be pregnant with his child now; you know, I'm a father figure for many of the children on my caseload." This victim felt the caseworker was saying that her stepfather would have eventually performed intercourse on her and impregnated her, and that she should be grateful to the caseworker because he had saved her. The victim was further shamed by this implication from the caseworker. Her stepfather had fondled her, and she'd had no thoughts of him performing intercourse on her and felt embarrassed that a caseworker would even suggest such a thing. Child protective services should be a support system, but obviously they were not supportive for this survivor.

Sadly, the mother in this case put her daughter in a risky situation where her daughter was allegedly raped by her mother's new boyfriend, and the mother did not believe her daughter's allegations. Her daughter is now fifteen and pregnant. The daughter asserted that she was unsure whether her pregnancy was from her own boyfriend or as a result of the alleged rape by her mother's boyfriend. John, the sex offender, was able to have the three children put in custody with his parents as a result of his victim's allegations against her mother's boyfriend. He was the more responsible parent, and took his step-daughter to the police when she alleged another sexual violation. Child protective services were also informed of the new allegations, and the children were placed with John's parents. He completed sex offender treatment, whereas the mother refused to complete a treatment program designed for the significant others of sex offenders, and she avoided addressing her addiction to alcohol and other drugs. The family's initial goal was to reunify. That required the mother's completion of the program for significant others, which would have helped her learn how to keep her children safe and recognize risk behaviors of sex offenders. She failed to complete the treatment and did not enter a substance abuse program. At this writing, the case is before the authorities, who plan to charge the mother with contributing to the delinquency of a minor, because she gave her daughter alcohol, and the mother's boyfriend with a sex crime.

It is not uncommon for mothers of teenage daughters to not believe their children, especially if the mother is abusing alcohol and other drugs, as in the previous case. Survivors need support systems that do not blame them or make excuses for the sex offenders, are sensitive to their emotions, and have the best interests of the survivor in mind.

A good support system for a sex offender includes someone who does not say things like: "I know you wouldn't do that"; "I know you didn't do that"; "I know you would never do that again; I trust you with my kids." No one—whether it is a spouse, parent, sibling, friend, neighbor, or religious leader—provides effective support to a sex offender by voicing such beliefs. A good support system for a sex offender includes someone who says, "I know you did this—and possibly more than what you are admitting to doing—and I am going to keep my eye on you and watch you carefully when you are in the presence of children." Too many sex offenders have so-called support systems that let them off the hook. A good support system for a sex offender includes individuals who will be suspicious of their behavior and keep an eye on them.

The Duration of the Sexual Assault

Some survivors are sexually assaulted once, whereas others are sexually assaulted multiple times over a number of years. One would probably assume that the longer the sexual violation endures, the more the survivors are impacted, but no one can say for sure. Some survivors are sexually violated for long periods of time and somehow heal, cope, and move on to have a healthy and full life. However, others who were sexually assaulted for shorter periods do not heal very well. While the duration of the sexual assault is a factor to be considered when addressing sexual violations, focusing on how the survivors were impacted and can heal is more important. What follows are two case examples. One victim was sexually assaulted only once, and the other was sexually assaulted repeatedly over eight years. Victims as well as significant others believe the offender should apologize for their behavior regardless of whether it happened once or over a period of years. These cases illustrate the need for an apology regardless of the duration of the sexual assault.

I worked with an adult survivor whose brother-in-law attempted to rape her and almost had her pants down before she was able to get away. This was an incident of very short duration with respect to the sexual assault itself, but it affected her more profoundly than other victims who were sexually abused over a period of years. She was one of the most emotionally distressed survivors with which I have worked. She kept saying she wanted an apology from her brother-in-law. I explained to her that he was an untreated, unconvicted sex offender, and if he did apologize, he was extremely likely to re-victimize her by blaming her for his actions and, once again, not taking full responsibility for his inappropriate behavior. Sex offenders cannot apologize without first admitting to themselves that they have sexually violated someone in addition to having had appropriate treatment. This survivor's expectation was unrealistic.

Unfortunately, many survivors mistakenly believe that sex offenders will admit to and apologize for their inappropriate behavior if confronted. If survivors do demand an apology from an untreated sex offender, they will probably be re-victimized. I worked with one adult survivor, Anne, who had demanded an apology from her untreated, unconvicted father, who she alleged had sexually assaulted her for at least eight years. She kept writing letters to her father, Jack, demanding he receive treatment. Anne received a call from Jack's individual therapist—who did not specialize in treating sex offenders—and a letter of apology from Jack. The letter was extremely re-victimizing, but, as a survivor, Anne did not recognize it as such.

Following is examples of statements made by this untreated, unconvicted sex offender, "I believe that we must look at why we do what we do." While this sounds good on the surface, it is re-victimizing because it implies that Anne was a willing participant in her own victimization. Sexual assault is not a "*we*" behavior. It is an adult abusing a child or an adult forcing himself on another adult.

The treatment of choice for sex offenders is group treatment. Individual therapy is not as effective because the sex offender may easily manipulate and deceive the therapist; whereas in group treatment offenders are able to confront one another about the way they are managing their lives in a deceptive manner. Sex offenders are unable to manipulate and deceive others as easily in group treatment and are more receptive to others who have engaged in similar behaviors. Jack had never been prosecuted and was in individual therapy. It is crucial that sex offenders attend group treatment with someone who specializes in the field. In group treatment, other offenders confront them with the ways they are placing themselves at risk of losing their freedom and not being truthful with themselves. Jack's response is typical of an untreated sex offender. Had he been in a sex offender program, he would probably not be asking himself why he sexually assaulted, but instead how he set it up and planned it, and he would have been more likely to take full responsibility for his behavior.

Anne had informed Jack of the grooming article by O'Connell. Having read this article, he continued to re-victimize her by denying that he groomed. All sex offenders groom their victims and others in some way regardless if they are able to identify and recognize it or not. All sex offenders are in some degree of denial when they begin treatment. According to Levenson and Morin (2000), they will deny the facts, their responsibility, the impact of their behavior, or their need for treatment. The following is an example of Jack's denial: "I was not grooming anyone, just doing a parental duty, as did others." It is unclear what exactly he meant by "doing a parental duty", but some sex offenders my colleague and I treated have believed it was their duty to teach their child about sex; therefore sexually abusing them. How does such denial help survivors? Moreover, how does this denial impact them? It sounds as if Jack is saying that his belief is many parents sexually violate their children.

One last example of Jack re-victimizing Anne was when he made reference to controlling his behavior: "As for my lack of control of my temper, I believe that to be a bad trait handed down to me, and which you have also received." Jack blames his temper on genetics, asserting that his behavior is not a matter of choice or self-control, and then judges and projects his behavior onto Anne by saying she has the same bad trait. Survivors already feel as if something is wrong with them after they have been sexually violated, and Jack reinforces that belief by implying that something is wrong with Anne.

It is very risky to request or demand an apology from an untreated sex offender. One of the ways Anne was impacted by Jack's sexual misconduct was her development of strong control issues. Sexual assault is about one human being having control and power over another and crossing sexual boundaries. It is easy to see why Anne, like most survivors, understandably developed some type of control issues. She tried to force Jack into treatment even though the statute of limitations had expired in the state where she alleged she had been sexually assaulted. She had an extremely difficult time stopping the impact of Jack's sexual abuse and may never stop it fully.

Sex offenders should be confronted by their therapeutic providers when they try to describe their sexual assault as something that "just happened." If this were the case, then sex offenders can not be treated. The idea that something "just happens" implies both a lack of control and intent. If sex offenders have no control over their behavior, then therapists are wasting their time attempting to treat sex offenders. "It just happened," is a way for sex offenders to avoid taking full responsibility for intentionally manipulating the situation to a point where they could commit a sexual offense. My colleague and I discuss with sex offenders that it is "something you did," not something that "just happened." However, it is something that "happens" to survivors, because they have no control over what is being done to them by the sex offender. Thus, whether the offender sexually assaulted one time or for an extended period, there is an impact some survivor will deal with throughout her life span.

3

Thinking Errors of Sex Offenders, Victims, and Significant Others

All sex offenders give themselves permission to sexually violate their victims. Once they recognize and admit how they gave themselves permission to offend sexually, they can begin to stop themselves should they begin giving themselves permission to sexually offend again. Sexually offending is not easy to explain or understand. It is complicated, inappropriate sexual behavior with which most people would prefer not to have to deal with. Survivors sometimes desperately want to understand why they were sexually offended. Trying to answer this question is probably not as helpful to them as working on placing responsibility on the sex offenders instead of blaming themselves. Sex offenders initially justify their inappropriate behavior by blaming the victim or their own circumstances, such as not having a job or marital problems or other family problems. Even when they do admit to their sexually offensive behavior, they can still be in partial denial, as indicated by their tendency to discuss irrelevant information and by focusing on the victim's behavior rather than focusing on their own deviant thinking and planning. For example, my colleague and I treated a law enforcement officer. The officer wanted us to look down on his victim, who he alleged was a "drug dealer and whore." Whether she was either or both, however, was irrelevant. What was relevant was that he had stood at his front door and intentionally exposed himself to her. He had to focus on how he set it up to expose himself and address his deviant thinking he used at the time while in treatment. Sex offenders will initially play dumb and make excuses for their behavior, while survivors will struggle with the question "Why me?"

All sex offenders should have to identify their offense pattern in treatment. An offense pattern is how they set the offense up, planned it, and acted it out. All sex offenders pick their targets, some with much thought, others more impulsively. Many personal events take place for sex offenders before they get to the point of acting out their criminal behavior. Emotional circumstances are present in the sex offenders' lives at the times they sexually offend. These circumstances could include negative feelings about themselves, failed relationships, inability to maintain jobs, isolation, use of pornography, deviant sexual habits or fantasies, drugs or alcohol abuse, regular access to children, a propensity to deceive or keep secrets from people, living a double life, or boredom. Instead of coping with whatever is going on in their lives, they begin planning a sex offense, thinking that it will make them feel better.

Others sexually offend because they are sexually attracted to children. How many professionals, wives, or other support persons could handle a man coming to them saying, "I am having sexual fantasies about my ten-year-old daughter?" Potential sex offenders visualize that if they do tell someone, their wives will leave, their clergy will throw them out of their religious institution, or their friends will hate them. They keep the fantasy a secret, eventually act on their thoughts, and may indeed experience their wives leaving, expulsion from their religious community, or the loss of their friends. Once they act out, they could face legal charges at some point because most states have no statute of limitations on sex offenses. Many sex offenders are not convicted at the time of their offense but years later when the victim discloses while many others are never convicted because victims under report. For those who are convicted of a sex offense, many not all are required to register as sex offender. Some are not required to register because of the plea bargain their attorney worked out in court. Would it have been better for them to talk about their deviant fantasy before they acted? The question is: Do we socialize individuals to discuss thoughts that involve illegal behavior? I have received several phone calls from young men who wanted to ask about my fee. I asked them why they wanted to come to therapy. They stated that they did not know why, but that they sometimes had perverse thoughts. I told them that was a very good reason to seek therapy, and, in fact, that they could possibly end up with legal problems if they did not seek therapy. They never came to me for therapy. I hope they saw someone else.

Victims are also guided by thinking errors. Once sex offenders have sexually violated their victims, victims adopt their own thinking errors in order to make sense of what happened to them. The sex offenders used thinking errors to give themselves permission to sexually violate, and now the survivors may have thinking errors, until they recognize them and change them. Mothers or other caretakers of the victims may also have thinking errors. Professional research on victims of sexual abuse gives examples of thinking errors for sex offenders, but is not as clear about what the sex offender should do with those thinking errors. In addition, the thinking errors of victims and significant others are not mentioned as often. First, offenders, significant others, and victims have to identify their thinking errors. Second, they have to correct them. Offenders and significant others will need to identify and correct their thinking errors in order to prevent further abuse, whereas victims will need to do so to heal and prevent further abuse. The following are some examples of thinking errors and corrected thinking. Because I can't read minds, there is no way I or anyone else could mention all thinking errors that are used *before*, *during*, or *after* a sex offense. I hope these examples will help people identify the thinking errors they frequently use to justify a sex offense or place blame on someone else.

Thinking Error	Corrected Thinking
Sex Offender:	
•She wanted it.	No one wants to be sexually assaulted.
•The same thing happened to me.	I had no right to sexually offend.
•I wasn't thinking at the time.	I was thinking about how to offend.
•It just happened.	It did not just happen; I planned it.
•It was a mistake.	This was intentional, not a mistake.
•I only did it once.	That is minimizing, I had no right—ever.
•I was set up.	I set up my victims and tricked them.
•It won't happen again.	I can always sexually re-offend.
•She didn't stop me.	I was supposed to stop me, and no one else.
•I didn't hurt her.	I hurt her and need to ponder that.
•She was putting out for others.	No matter what I thought, I had no right to touch her.
•I loved her.	I used her and confused her about love.
•Children like it.	Children like appropriate touching and affection.
•She was wet and liked it.	The body responds to sexual stimulation; that does not mean she liked it.
•She was walking around in her underwear and shaking her butt.	It was my responsibility to leave the situation rather than let myself get sexually aroused.

<u>Thinking Error</u>	<u>Corrected Thinking</u>
<u>Sex Offender:</u>	
•I taught her about sex.	It is not my responsibility to teach minors about sex.
•She got in my bed.	My responsibility was to leave the bedroom.
•She sat in my lap to turn me on.	She sat in my lap for affection, not to sexually arouse me.
•She didn't tell for days/months/ years.	Children do not tell for various reasons, such as fear of not being believed and other reasons I need to consider.
•It wasn't planned.	All sex offenders plan their offense, whether it takes 5 minutes or years. I planned mine.
•I didn't mean to do it.	I did mean to do it. I have to pay attention to my behavior the rest of my life.
•She didn't say no.	She said no in ways to which I did not pay attention.
•I didn't penetrate.	I am minimizing the harm I caused when I say this.
•I'll never do this again.	I am at risk to re-offend for the rest of my life.
•It was a joke.	Sexually touching a child is not a joke, it is criminal behavior.
•No one will know.	She will eventually tell.
•I deserved it.	It is only permissible to have consensual sexual contact with adults.

Thinking Error	Corrected Thinking
Survivor:	
•No one will believe me.	Someone will eventually believe me.
•He didn't mean to do it.	He meant it and planned it, even though I did not recognize it.
•I let him.	I was tricked. No one lets someone sexually violate them.
•I'll break up the family if I tell.	He broke up the family, not me.
•There was something wrong with me.	His behavior was wrong, not mine.
•No one will want me now.	People can see the good in me that I miss, and they can't see that I was offended.
•I am dirty.	I did nothing dirty; he was inappropriate.
•I am lesser than others.	I am not lesser than others; he did wrong.
•I can't enjoy sex.	I can heal and learn to enjoy sex as an adult.
•People know I was sexually violated.	No one can see that, even if it feels that way.
•I have to keep secrets.	I can learn to be open.

Thinking Error	Corrected Thinking
Survivor:	
•It was my fault.	It was his fault, because he took advantage of me sexually.
•I consented.	In many states, no one can consent if under 16. If there is a 3-year age difference in many states there can be a sex charge.

Thinking Error	Corrected Thinking
Mothers/Significant Others:	
• He wouldn't do that.	He did it; he set it up, and now I have to deal with it.
•This has been blown out of proportion.	I am minimizing; recognizing inappropriate sexual touching is not blowing it out of proportion.
•The general statutes say breasts are not sex organs.	I know breasts are sexual organs; I am making excuses.
•He won't do it again.	He is always at risk to re-offend.
•She lies all the time.	Children seldom lie about sex offenses. I am not holding him responsible when I say this.
•She said this because she was mad.	She may have been mad, but that does not mean he was not sexually violating her.
•She snuck out of the house and had sex with him.	He was the older one, and it was his responsibility to have called me, the mother, no matter what.
•I had no idea he was doing this.	I need to look at things that were wrong in the relationship and suspicions that I ignored.
•He's not a criminal.	He committed a crime, even if he never gets convicted.

As stated before, it is impossible for me or anyone else to identify all the thinking errors people use when forced to address a sexual offense. Many people will choose to never change their thinking errors, regardless of subsequent treatment or education. They would rather believe their thinking error than challenge it, such as those men who are members of the North American Man Boy Love Association (NAMBLA). This organization has their own views regarding sexual contact between adults and minors, just like many individuals have their own beliefs about sexual contact with minors, and I believe no amount of literature could change certain people's thinking errors.

However, it is important, whether you are a survivor, mother, sex offender, significant other, or professional, to challenge your thinking errors. What sex offenders tell themselves can give them permission to commit a sex offense. What significant others tell themselves can help them fail to recognize dangerous behavior and prevent abuse. What victims tell themselves can keep them depressed and limit their emotional well-being.

Many seventeen- and eighteen-year-old males are charged with sex offenses, and their justification for their actions is often that the girls told them they were sixteen when they were actually younger. Treatment in sex offender programs should focus on the sex offenders' poor judgment and lack of responsibility in developing relationships. One eighteen-year-old, Mark, wanted us to collaborate with him in blaming his victim. His story was that the girl told him she was sixteen, pulled her pants down, and asked him if he wanted some. Just as he was about to touch her, the police came running by them from a nearby criminal investigation. The police saw them, and Mark was arrested and charged with a sex crime. Of course, his therapy group members confronted him about his inability to take responsibility, even though the girl's behavior was inappropriate. Mark is only in the early stages of treatment and is not yet aware of his thinking errors. Identifying and working through thinking errors takes time, but it is a necessary part of the work sex offenders need to do to help prevent themselves from sexually re-offending. They also need to return to therapy whenever they find themselves having thinking errors again before re-offending.

Survivors need to challenge their thinking errors in order to heal and stop verbally battering or otherwise hurting themselves for the behavior of others. Also, if survivors challenge their own thinking errors, they can help protect their children or other children they may be around from sexual abuse. One mother, Michele, had the following thinking error: "He did it to me, but he won't do it to my daughter." Her father had sexually abused her and went to prison for sexually abusing her daughter. Had she corrected her thinking before the offense against her daughter, she may have prevented her daughter from being sexually abused. The good news is that it is never too late to correct thinking errors. Michele can work on identifying any other thinking errors she may have and correct them. It is possible for her to prevent her grandchildren from being sexually assaulted. In this case, Michele was both a survivor and a significant other. Significant others need to challenge their thinking errors in order to have a better understanding of reality and increase their protection skills. Likewise, if significant others fully examine their own beliefs and the falsehoods they tell themselves, then children can be safer.

4

Similarities Between Sex Offenders and Survivors: Self-Blame, Keeping Secrets, Risk Situations, Denial, Promiscuity, Victimization

Survivors in particular may find the idea of similarities with sex offenders very disturbing. The topic is not something I have read about in the literature on the subject matter. It is not an area that people want to discuss or think about.

I would have never thought about the similarities between survivors and sex offenders when I was working at a rape crisis center and found sex offenders repulsive. It was only when I began treating sex offenders in an outpatient community setting that I began to think about the similarities between the two. I became interested in treating sex offenders for several reasons. One was to help their victims. Survivors do not want the person who sexually assaulted them to offend again. When treating sex offenders, I have an opportunity to present survivors' viewpoints and to challenge sex offenders to see their behavior from the survivors' perspectives instead of their own. A second reason was to help survivors understand more clearly what was done to them. Having listened to sex offenders' absurd attempts to justify their behaviors, I am better able to help survivors identify when they are dialoguing in a fashion that is similar to sex offenders', such as blaming themselves. For example, sex offenders entering treatment will state that the victims did not say no. Victims will also begin treatment by explaining that they did not say no. At that time, I discuss the ways they said no with their nonverbal body language, and that victims say no frequently without verbally saying no. Victims then give me examples of how they said no and were trying to convey that they did not want to be touched in a sexual manner.

Self-Blame

Sex offenders and survivors both tend to blame the survivor. Initially, sex offenders blame the survivors in some manner. They can be admitting that they sexually violated the victims while, at the same time, blaming them, which indicates that they do not take full responsibility for their sex offenses.

One sex offender committed his crime at age seventeen to a fourteen-year-old. They were in group homes following removal from their homes by social services. This sex offender had been in treatment for approximately a year and had transferred to my treatment program. The therapist and group members thought he would be past blaming his survivor, but he began explaining his offense pattern with, "We did this." The other group members stopped him and pointed out that sex offenses are not a "we act."

In treating survivors, helping them work through their tendency to blame themselves is difficult. My observation has been that survivors struggle with blaming themselves more than sex offenders struggle with not blaming the survivors. This could be in part because, upon disclosure, all parties involved—whether it is their mother, the police, social services, or their friends—tend to blame the survivors. If others do not actually blame the victims, they are suspicious of the victims' allegations.

Society has a history of blaming females. Even though there is a greater tendency to believe younger children today, teens and older victims are still frequently blamed. I once worked with a grandmother who had custody of her four-year-old grandchild. The four-year-old had been sexually abused by her mother and her mother's boyfriend. The grandmother could only focus on the child's flirtatiousness and "the way she pranced around in front of men." Obviously, this child had been sexualized, but whose responsibility was it to instruct her in nonverbal behavior? The grandmother talked about this as if the child was purposely doing this and had a concept of her behavior. In essence, the grandmother was blaming the child.

The video *Breaking the Silence* shows four children in therapy talking about having been physically, sexually, and emotionally abused by adults. For the ten-year-old female survivor of sexual abuse, near the end of her story she states, "I know I will never let anyone do this to me again." The point is she did not let anyone do this to her, and the implication of her statement is that she had a part in the sex offender's behavior. As an adult, will she still be saying that she let an adult sexually abuse her when she was a child? This is highly possible, and is true of many adult abuse cases I work today. Until survivors stop blaming themselves, treatment is incomplete.

Sex offenders blame the survivors when they comment on sexy or revealing clothing the victims were wearing. Many sex offenders do this regardless of the age of the children. I have heard a number of sex offenders who assaulted girls age twelve or younger say, "She was walking around in a T-shirt and panties." My response is, "What is your responsibility, to sit there and let yourself get sexually aroused, or to remove yourself from the situation and talk to the proper adult about the situation?" Sex offenders blame survivors when they imply that the victims initiated the sexual abuse. For example, offenders might say, "She got in the bed." In most cases, the survivors' behavior is irrelevant because of the age difference. Sex offenders blame survivors when they say, "She told me she was eighteen." Children's behavior is not as relevant as adult behavior. The issue is: What is the responsibility of the adult offenders?

I briefly treated one sex offender, Joseph, who claimed that he had been responsible in that he had gotten to know the girl's parents, and they wanted him around. Joseph, who was in his late twenties, was living with this family, who had a daughter under sixteen. He said he had no other place to live. After he had been charged with a sex crime, he wanted the group members to feel sorry for him because this family had done the same thing to other men, which in his mind was to get men to live there and then cry rape of their daughter.

Nevertheless, despite the role of the family's attitude, it is important to recognize that it was, after all, Joseph's responsibility to avoid committing a sex crime against a minor. He manipulated himself out of the sex offender treatment program with the approval of his probation officer and is at risk of re-offending in the future. According to Karl Hanson's research, not completing treatment is a higher risk to re-offend than denial of the offense. No matter what these parents did, no matter what the daughter did, had Joseph been responsible, he would have recognized the risk inherent in the situation.

Keeping Secrets

Sex offenders commit their sex offenses in secret so as not to get caught, not to have legal problems, and to keep fooling others into thinking that they are outstanding citizens. On the other hand, survivors keep their abuse secret out of shame, fear of being blamed, fear of not being believed, fear of breaking up the family, fear of being killed by the sex offender, and the fear of family members not loving them. Both have to learn to talk about their secrets. Survivors face the challenge of finding someone they can trust who will not judge them or blame them. Survivors who try to talk with their spouses sometimes hear, "You were old enough to know better." This is not a supportive response, and keeps the survivors shut down, because they will expect these same kinds of remarks from others, including therapists. Survivors have to learn with whom they can safely discuss the sexual assault.

Sex offenders, however, will not talk about their secrets until they are in treatment and are confronted with how they tricked and fooled others. They have to learn that they cannot keep secrets. They also have to learn how to be open. Sex offender treatment includes having offenders identify how they are managing their lives in ways to continue practicing deception and keeping secrets. We had one sex offender who decided to get married without telling the group. He knew that this meant he was keeping a secret, and eventually told the group he got married. The group members confronted him about his keeping the marriage a secret. They have to learn to use the group before making decisions rather than after the fact. Within three months he found himself consulting the group about his marital problems and upcoming divorce. Another sex offender got married and separated without telling the group. Keeping secrets takes more energy than being open.

Failure to Identify Risk Situations

When treating sex offenders, risk situations are discussed frequently, because sex offenders often put themselves in risky situations where they might be tempted to re-offend or be accused of doing so. One sex offender decided he was going to go to the mayor of his local city on behalf of the National Football League and head up a charity event for a cancer survivor. He would be at a function with many children and adults around. If the sex offender is fully participating in treatment, he will inform the group and providers of his intentions and ask for suggestions. Fortunately, this sex offender did bring his intentions up, whereupon I asked him if he had informed the NFL that he was a registered sex offender. I also presented the following scenario to him: Suppose that he had not told anyone, and he went to the mayor, and someone saw his picture with the mayor in the paper and called the mayor and informed the mayor that he was photographed with a registered sex offender. He was advised to inform the NFL of his status in the community. When he did inform the NFL, they restricted some of the plans he had and limited his involvement in the fundraiser. He was a sex offender, and the group expected him to have recognized this risky behavior and thought it through before making the plans. He gave himself permission to engage in this risky behavior by using the thinking error that he had headed another charity event in his community where the police were present and no problems arose; therefore, he assumed no problems would arise from this event.

Survivors tend to be naïve; they are unaware of how sex offenders plan their offenses and often interpret a sex offender's behavior as being no different than that of a "nice guy." Because many sex offenders do nice things for their victims, such as buying gifts, taking them to functions or spending time with them when no one else is there for them, victims fail to see the set up. The younger the child, the more difficult it is to detect alarming behavior. On the other hand, adults fail to recognize risk situations and are expected to do this more so than children. One rapist my colleague and I treated gave a victim a ride home from a bar one evening. She was very violently raped. She believed he was being a nice guy by agreeing to take her home, which was naïve. As far as criminal behavior goes, except for their sexual misconduct, many sex offenders are some of the most law-abiding citizens in society. Many times they have no criminal record.

Children under the age of twelve who are sexually assaulted may have a sense of certain situations being a risk, but they do not have the skills to verbalize a situation as a risk. This is frequently due to the grooming behavior of the sex offenders and their awareness that young children do not have sexual knowledge. Children under twelve are easier to manipulate and coerce than older victims. Teens and young women frequently do not recognize risk situations at parties, bowling alleys, skating rinks, movies, sorority and fraternity parties, or other places. Survivors tend not to recognize the use of alcohol and other drugs as a risk situation for sexual assault, whereas offenders use the alcohol and other drugs as an excuse not to take responsibility for their behavior.

One sex offender in treatment had sexually offended a twelve-year-old girl by exposing himself. He could tell us everything about the night in question, for example, how many people were there, how much beer they were drinking, what kind of drugs were being used, who was sleeping where, the child's clothing, and her behavior, but he could not remember exposing himself. He said that this twelve-year-old was flirting with him. He also talked about her sleeping position, which he had sexualized; he believed in his mind that she was deliberately sleeping in a sexual position to tease him. This sex offender did not recognize the risk situation he was in until after he had sexually offended.

Before entering a situation, teens and young women need to ask themselves whether this is a place where they could potentially be sexually assaulted. Men need to ask themselves whether this is a situation where they could sexually offend or be accused of sexually offending. For younger children, it is an adult's responsibility to make sure they are not placed in situations where they can be sexually assaulted.

The stepfather in a family I worked with went into his fourteen-year-old stepdaughter's room while she was asleep at night and touched her breast; at that time, she woke up. How did the stepfather get to the point where he gave himself permission to do this? The family would go shopping together, the mother would go off by herself, and the child would go with her stepfather to try on bathing suits and other clothing. This is when he began looking at her in a sexual manner, long before he ever touched her. None of them saw this as a risk situation. Untreated, sex offenders will not recognize risk situations, but once sex offenders have had treatment, they should always ask themselves: "Is this a situation where I have an opportunity to re-offend or be accused of re-offending?" If the answer is yes, then it is in their best interest to replace the situation with something appropriate and positive.

Survivors seem to find it more difficult to recognize risk situations than sex offenders who have had treatment. Survivors tend not to realize the risks until they are caught in the situation, and it is too late then. For example, I worked with a seventeen-year-old, Charity, who found herself in a situation of attempted rape. She came to me after reporting the incident to the police. Clearly, she did not see her decision as putting herself at risk. She and a friend agreed to go with two males in their twenties at 2:00 AM to their house. Charity was staying overnight with the friend and discussed how easy it was to sneak out because her friend's mother did not pay attention. Both men attempted to rape both of them. Granted, this was not the best decision these two teens could have made; however, the men were considered adults and would be held liable for their behavior even though the teens' behavior was questionable. Fortunately, they were able to get out of this situation, and no rape took place. By contrast, sex offenders plan their acts and do not believe they will get caught, nor do they recognize how they are giving themselves permission to sexually offend at the time.

Denial

Survivors and sex offenders both deny aspects of the sexual assault. Survivors deny aspects of the sexual assault because of the shame of discussing what was done to them. Sometimes they deny having been sexually assaulted because they do not want to believe they have been victims of a sex crime. Often they do not even recognize that they are victims of a sexual assault but simply view the incident as sex they did not want. They do not understand that what happened to them was a sex crime. If these survivors admitted to themselves that they were sexually assaulted, then they would see themselves as weak.

I worked with a survivor who had been raped, and as she and the rapist were walking back to the car, he stabbed her in the back. She would refer to this as, "When I had my accident." I gently confronted her on this by saying, "Accident?" in a shocked manner. This was no accident, but planned behavior on the part of the sex offender; however, it was easier for the victim to say to herself that she had an accident than that she had been stabbed. This was part of her denial about what had happened to her. Eventually she became able to say, "When he stabbed me."

Sex offenders deny having sexually offended for various reasons: for fear of being labeled a pervert or of being physically assaulted; to avoid their wife leaving: to avoid getting a criminal record (if they do not already have one); to prevent being ostracized; and fear of losing their jobs, families, and friends.

According to Levenson and Morin, sex offenders and significant others have a tendency to deny in the following ways:

•The sex offender denies the facts by saying, "I didn't do it," and the significant other denies by saying, "He didn't do it."

•The sex offender denies awareness by blaming alcohol or other drugs, and the significant other states that he or she was away at work, and the victim never explained what happened.

•The sex offender denies responsibility by blaming the child, saying, "She wanted sex," and the significant other states, "The child came on to him."

•The sex offender denies harm by saying, "I didn't hurt her," and the significant other says, "She will get over it...."

•The sex offender denies the need for treatment by saying, "I learned my lesson, I'll never do it again," and the significant other states, "He's scared of her now; He won't do that again."

Applying Levenson and Morin's denial of sex offenders and significant others, survivors have a tendency to deny the facts of the abuse in the following ways:

•They may change their story by deleting facts. One fifteen-year-old I worked with who was sexually assaulted by her biological father and stepfather denied her stepfather had performed intercourse on her in the hopes that he would get to come back home, because she believed she split up the family. Her mother denied that her second husband was sexually abusing her daughter and did not believe it until she walked in on him sexually abusing her.

•They may deny responsibility. Survivors think they should have been able to stop the offenders. Rarely can children stop adults from touching them in a sexual manner. What they don't realize is that they did stop it when they dis-

Similarities Between Sex Offenders and Survivors: Self-Blame, Keeping
Secrets, Risk Situations, Denial, Promiscuity, Victimization

41

closed. However, in the case of those survivors who did not disclose to anyone and for whom the abuse stopped for any number of reasons, they continue to struggle in adulthood with the idea of not having stopped the abuse themselves. They do not think that the sex offender should have stopped, instead of them having to stop it. In rape situations, if the survivors try to stop it, they run the risk of being harmed more. They deny the offender's responsibility.

•They may deny harm. This is truer for younger survivors than adult survivors. They deny they were hurt and say it does not bother them.

•They may deny the need for treatment. Survivors deny that they need any treatment and maintain that they are handling the situation and are unaware of how it affects their everyday life.

Become Promiscuous

Some survivors and sex offenders become promiscuous. Survivors become promiscuous for various reasons. Some are searching for the feeling of self-worth that they lost when they were sexually violated. They want to be valued as human beings rather than as sex objects, thus they have sex with many different people thinking that at some point they will find someone who cares about them for themselves instead of just for sex. Some survivors are promiscuous because they are confused about sex and love. They believe that sex is a way for them to get love, and often sex offenders have told them that this is a way of showing them love. This goes along with the thinking error they adopt from sex offenders.

Male sex offenders may become promiscuous because they want to prove their manhood. Others feel inadequate and believe that this feeling will go away if they have sex with enough people. Some are promiscuous simply because sex is running their lives, and they place too much emphasis on sex. At some point both survivors and sex offenders may stop being promiscuous because they want to change, they get their needs met in more healthy ways, get married, or because they have caught a number of sexually transmitted diseases. Others never change their sexual behavior.

Failure to Recognize Self as a Victim

In today's open society, girls in particular can be victims of a sexual assault without recognizing it. For years, some boys who have been victims of sexual assaults have not recognized the incidents as such. I worked with a fourteen-year-old girl, Jenny, who would sneak out of her house to engage in sex by a twenty-four-year-old. She saw nothing wrong with this, and was brought to me after he had been charged with a sex crime against her. She was determined not to testify against him. Jenny first had sex when she was thirteen by a seventeen-year-old who died a week later in an automobile accident. In this state, an individual can potentially be charged with a sex crime if there is a three-year age difference. The laws in each state need to be clarified regarding age difference for a criminal charge. Because she was thirteen, she was not of legal age to consent to sex. Many teens in schools today are sexually active and are uninformed about the age of consent. She did not recognize her first sexual experience as a sex crime. She stated that the police had read the current sex offender's criminal record to her. I asked her what she remembered about that. Her response was, "Oh, nothing bad, robbery, assaulting his mother, and the L word." I asked her if she meant larceny, and she said yes. She did not think any of this was bad. She talked about how much the offender had told her that he loved her. She did not see herself as a victim of a sex crime, but believed this was more about love. How will she look at this when she is forty years old? She may not yet understand how she will be affected differently later in life.

For example, a woman was referred to me by her primary care physician for depression. She had entered therapy because of marital problems: both of her ex-husbands had had affairs. She was a single mother raising her then ten-year-old daughter. She would say, "There are things I will not talk to anyone about." She would not be pushed, due to her defensiveness. She presented to me over a three-year period, but would only discuss so much. Over the three-year period, she attended eight or fewer sessions a year. In the third year, she was able to discuss having been impregnated by an eighteen-year-old when she was fifteen years old. She gave the child up for adoption to a relative. The relative would not have anything to do with her afterwards, nor allow her to have contact with the child even though she never felt a connection to the child. While she was attending therapy, the child discovered who his mother was. I processed what happened to her, and for the first time in her life she could verbalize she had been taken advantage of sexually. Now she is deciding how to deal with her son's questions regarding his father. She did some searching because she believed the father had gone to an attorney and had given up parental rights. When she contacted the attorney, she discovered that what she had thought for twenty years was incorrect. He did not relinquish parental rights; he signed papers denying he ever knew her. Fortunately, DNA can easily answer that question today, and he could possibly be charged with a sex crime should she decide to pursue the matter further. She feels this has contributed to her depression, defensiveness, and poor relationships with people in general.

I treated Tim, a sex offender who talked about his first sexual experience at age sixteen by a thirty-seven-year-old married woman who gave him alcohol during the months she sexually violated him. He thought her behavior was wonderful. When he found himself in sex offender group treatment and was asked how this first sexual experience had impacted his life, he was in denial that this could be a reason he was promiscuous. He had contracted many venereal diseases, and in treatment did not initially see anything wrong with attempting to perform sex acts on a thirteen-year-old girl when he was in his mid twenties; he served prison time for this offense. He had managed his life in such a manner that he was driving while intoxicated on a number of occasions, to the point of losing his license. When he was about eight, Tim's father had kidnapped him from his mother, who had custody of him. Tim thought this was acceptable behavior by his father. His mother could not find him for about four years, but his father was never prosecuted. When confronted about what kind of lessons he had learned from adults, and what kinds of lessons he was going to teach his newborn son, he began to think about impact; however, he never saw himself as a victim of a sex crime and chose to remain in denial about that. Clearly Tim was a victim, which helped him fail to recognize when he was hurting others because he did not see himself as having been harmed.

Others who are likely not to recognize themselves as victims of a sex crime are children and adolescents who meet sex offenders through the Internet. These victims tell police investigators that they wanted to have sex; this was their first love; they had it all planned out. In the county where I live, a female sex offender was recently arrested for luring a teenage boy over state lines for sexual purposes. I wonder if this adolescent sees himself as a victim of a sex crime or as someone who had a sexually exciting experience he will never forget.

A widely publicized case was that of Mary Kay Letourneau. She was a schoolteacher, married, with four children, who sexually abused her male student and was impregnated by this eighth grader. The judge in this case believed her when she said she would not have any further contact with him and allowed her to be on probation, but she became pregnant a second time by the same adolescent. She had violated her probation by having contact with him when she was ordered not to and was imprisoned. What will be the impact on this boy? Does he see himself as a victim of a sex crime or as in love? Obviously he sees himself as in love since they married, but what will time tell?

5

Treatment for Survivors, Sex Offenders, Significant Others

Although the treatment recommendations that follow may look simple and methodical, they are not. Treatment is intense, complex, and long-term. The treatment of choice for sex offenders is group treatment. Victims benefit and heal faster when in group treatment, but they are more reluctant to attend group and cannot be compelled. Significant others are oftentime ordered by child protective services to attend group treatment. In Tables 1 and 2 you will see available treatment options for sex offenders, survivors, mothers, and significant others. Due to their manipulation skills, sex offenders can benefit greatly from the questions, comments, and confrontational opinions of other sex offenders who have progressed in treatment and will confront new sex offenders about their denial and manipulation in treatment. They will give incoming sex offenders examples of how they justified their offense or statements they made when they entered treatment to avoid taking responsibility for their behavior. This helps those offenders begin to take responsibility for their behavior and to examine their thinking errors. They also give examples of how they harmed not only their victim but also secondary victims: their wives, the victims' friends, family members, the community, and so forth. This helps those sex offenders begin to identify how much harm they did. For sex offenders, treatment takes approximately two years and often longer. It depends on whether the offenders are taking the treatment seriously, or continuing their pattern of deception, which obviously prolongs the treatment.

One thing of which survivors are unaware is that many sex offenders enter treatment in partial or full denial. Historically, many sex offender programs would not accept offenders who were in denial, although this is changing. My program accepts deniers because it is likely they committed the crime and will eventually admit to their sex offense. I once did an assessment for a sex offender who denied he even knew the person who had made allegations against him. He wanted me to find this woman so he could meet her. Eventually, he admitted that she worked for him. He said he would get her into his office alone, which is when he touched her in a sexual manner. If anyone is found guilty of a sex crime, they should receive treatment, whether they are admitting or denying. In treatment, sex offenders are expected to address their offense pattern, which (as mentioned earlier) is how they gave themselves permission to sexually offend. The offense pattern is explored to do the following: determine the way they set up and planned the sex offense; identify their thinking errors used to sexually offend; identify risk situations where they could re-offend or be accused of re-offending; identify how they harmed their victim, which is the most difficult thing for a sex offender to do; and develop a *relapse-prevention plan* so that they will hopefully avoid future offenses and sign a *child safety protection plan*. A relapse-prevention plan details the steps that offenders can take when they catch themselves beginning to plan re-offenses. They can look at this as a reminder of what to do to prevent re-offending. The child safety protection plan provides a list of boundaries that offenders agree to use to govern the rest of their lives when they are around children so that they can behave safely.

Sex offender treatment does not just involve their present sex offense; it also involves sex offenders addressing the way they manage their lives. If they are in fact not guilty of a sex offense as they profess, then they have to address how they lived their lives in such a manner that they were accused of a sex offense and how they put themselves in a position where the only two choices they had were to plead guilty to a sex crime or go to trial and possibly be found guilty and go to prison. Once someone is indicted, they have to take a plea bargain or go to trial. Some sex offenders are allowed to take an Alford Plea (which is not an admission of guilt but recognizes there is enough evidence to convict), or plead guilty to Assault on a Female or Assault and Battery of a High and Aggravated Nature when in reality their crime was a sex offense. They were charged with a sex crime but pled down to one of the above. They will come to treatment and say I did not do anything, I was convicted of Assault on a Female or took an Alford Plea; I don't have to admit anything. In essence, if they did not do anything, they decided to plead guilty and if they violate their probation they will likely go to prison for what they were charged with not what they pled guilty to. They know they were charged with a sex offense and pled guilty to a lesser charge but want to come to treatment and act innocent, but they are confronted with pretending to be sex offenders when they took a plea bargain if in fact they are innocent, which means they need more treatment than sex offenders who admit to the charges against them. "Predictors of Sexual Offense Recidivism," by Karl Hanson (1998), cites denial as a lesser risk factor for a re-offense than not completing treatment. When we work with groups of sex offenders, my colleague and I often ask them, "Where is your victim?" "Where will she be when she is an adult?" "What kind of treatment is she getting?"

I treated a victim who stated that her stepfather had performed sexual intercourse on her, and she had previously been sexually abused by her biological father. Her stepfather served four years in prison. When he was released, he was referred to my sex offender treatment program. He knew that I had provided services for his victim; however, I did not acknowledge this because I did not have a release to discuss her with him. I knew that this victim had not received the treatment she needed. Her mother only brought her a few times, and she was a teen and did not resolve anything that had happened to her. Victims cannot be forced to attend treatment the way that offenders can, even though they need the treatment. Maybe this victim will return to treatment as an adult to deal with what happened to her or maybe she will never get any further treatment. My colleague and I discuss with sex offenders the irony that sex offenders resist treatment, but receive quality care, while their victims may never receive help. In most states, survivors do not have knowledge that if sex offenders are convicted, the court can order them to pay for their victims' treatment. Survivors can consult with their victim witness coordinators in their state to verify whether a court order was issued for their treatment. This can be done by contacting the local district attorney's office, which will direct them to the victim witness coordinator. In addition, survivors often do not take advantage of payment for treatment by Victim Assistance in their state. If victims do attend treatment due to sexual assaults that have been adjudicated, they can be reimbursed for any payments by filing the correct paperwork with Victim Assistance, which is obtained through the victim witness coordinator.

Survivors cannot be ordered by a court to attend treatment, whereas sex offenders attend treatment mostly by a court order. Many survivors do, however, elect to receive treatment, though a number of them do not complete the process because it is difficult work that can take months or years. Survivors sometimes stay in treatment much longer than sex offenders. Resolving the impact of sexual abuse must proceed at the survivors' pace and as they are ready. If they are not ready to deal with the assault, they may visit a therapist for several sessions and not return. Many survivors who were sexually abused as young children do not enter therapy until they are adults. Children who enter therapy are limited by their developmental and cognitive abilities in processing what happened to them, thus it is recommended they re-enter therapy as adults if the sexual assault starts to bother them.

Mothers or caretakers seldom enter therapy because their child or adolescent has been sexually assaulted. Child protective services frequently recommend that they do so, but the caretakers seldom follow through on it. My county has a group called Family Matters that does group work with the mothers or significant others of minors who have been sexually assaulted. Some mothers attend because they are ordered by the court through child protective services, but they sometimes resist attendance because they see it as an insult, instead of a source of help. Others attend because they want to be a supporter in helping offenders avoid re-offending or because they want to reunify with sex offenders in their family. The aim of the group is to help them learn more effective ways to protect their children and recognize signs they missed when their children were sexually assaulted. Mothers tend neither to want to address sexual assault nor accept any culpability. These are the most difficult populations to convince of their need for treatment. They are willing to bring their children, but unwilling to discuss any role they may have had in their child having been sexually assaulted. Many mothers of children who have been sexually violated were sexually violated themselves, and, in many of these cases, the mothers have never received treatment for their own victimization. The case I discussed previously concerning Sue is an instance of this. Sue had been sexually assaulted and had never dealt with her own victimization, but was more than willing to bring her daughter Holly to therapy to discuss her daughter's victimization.

In considering some areas of treatment that can be helpful for anyone affected by a sexual offense, do not be misled by how simplistic the treatment may seem. It is not a process of going through eleven steps, and then everyone is safe. These are very difficult questions to answer in depth. Sex offenders, survivors, and significant others benefit most from being in a group and discussing current life situations that might be an example of one of the steps of treatment. Step number five (under sex offenders) is "Take full responsibility for your behavior without blaming anything or anyone else." One sex offender, Terry, who had been in treatment for three months, was taking partial—not full—responsibility for his offense. He preferred to focus on her having a fake ID claiming she was nineteen rather than focus on the fact that he had been responsible for performing intercourse on her. After having obtained the police report that included his statement and the victim's statement, nothing was mentioned by either of them about a fake ID. In treatment he failed to inform the group that he had gone and brought three girls to his home, given them alcohol, and performed intercourse on one of them. He wanted to focus on one event—that she had called him and asked him to come over and watch movies—rather than on his behavior. Sex offenders take full responsibility when they talk about their offenses without mentioning their victims' behavior. This frequently takes months to realize. For survivors, step number three ("Identify patterns of behavior you engage in since the sexual violation.") could take months. Likewise, any step for caretakers (whether they are parents, grandparents, or significant others), survivors, or sex offenders could take months.

Table 1 What treatment looks like for survivors and sex offenders.

SEX OFFENDERS	SURVIVORS
1. Identify how you gave yourself permission to sexually violate.	1. Identify how you were manipulated, forced, or coerced.
2. Identify the thinking errors you used to sexually offend.	2. Identify thinking errors you have adopted since the sexual offense.
3. Identify your offense pattern (the way you planned it).	3. Identify patterns of behavior you engage in related to the offense.
4. Identify your emotions at the time you offended and other problem areas in your life at the time.	4. Deal with your feelings of shame, guilt, anger, or embarrassment.
5. Take full responsibility for your behavior without blaming or focusing on anyone else's behavior.	5. Hold the offender/s responsible and stop blaming yourself.
6. Write an apology letter to the victim and a victim empathy letter (not to be given to anyone).	6. Write a letter to the offender, mother, or any other person (not to be given).
7. Identify risk situations where you could re-offend or be accused of re-offending	7. Identify risky situations where you do not feel safe.
8. Identify how you harmed your victim/s and others.	8. Identify how you were harmed and impacted.
9. Follow the child safety protection plan.	9. Follow the child safety protection plan.

Table 1 What treatment looks like for survivors and sex offenders. (Continued)

SEX OFFENDERS	SURVIVORS
10. Make a relapse prevention plan to decrease your risk of re-offending.	10. Decide how you want to heal from the sexual violation/s and move forward.
11. Obtain a supporter who will not allow you to be in risky situations, be suspicious of your behavior, and keep an eye on you.	11. Obtain a supporter who will be sensitive and encouraging, but at the same time not let you feel sorry for yourself.

Table 2 Treatment for mothers, caretakers & significant others.

1. Identify any blind spots you may have had and how you missed your child or a child being sexually violated.

2. Identify thinking errors used to dismiss suspicious behavior.

3. Identify problems you were having at the time (marriage, financial, other).

4. Decide whether to continue or discontinue your relationship with the sex offender.

5. Take full responsibility for anything you may have done to fail to protect.

6. Address your feelings of guilt, anger, shame, or any others you may have.

7. Give your child an apology with the assistance of a therapist.

8. Follow the child safety protection plan.

9. Identify how your child or other victims were harmed

10. Obtain a supporter who knows all the facts and will help you identify risks.

6

Preventing and Assessing Sexual Misconduct

Preventing sexual misconduct is difficult. Many adults do not consider behaviors they engage in with children risky. However, there are some behaviors that should not be permitted, which can reduce the potential for a sexual re-offense by known sex offenders. Abiding by clear boundaries is a way to protect children and keep them safe. Unfortunately, many individuals perceive the following boundaries, which will be discussed to be too restrictive. (Levenson & Morin, 2000) developed some boundaries designed for sex offenders who will be reunifying with their family. Some of them are quoted hereafter, beginning with guideline number five.

5. Offender will never be responsible for babysitting or supervising children.

6. Discipline of the children will be done primarily by the nonoffending caretaker.

7. Offender will not discuss sex or dating with the children.

8. Physical affection between offender and children will be brief and will avoid bodily contact.

9. Physical hygiene assistance is always to be done by the nonoffending caretaker. This includes bathing, dressing, diapering, toileting.

10. There will be no tickling or wrestling between offender and children.

11. Offender will not have secrets with any child.

12. Offender will never enter the children's bedroom alone.

13. Offender will never enter the bathroom while a child is in it, nor will offender allow a child to enter the bathroom while he is in it.

14. All bedroom and bathroom doors will have locks.

15. If mutually agreed, children will be permitted to lock doors.

16. All family members will sleep in their own beds.

17. All family members bathe, shower, and toilet separately.

18. No family member shall enter a bathroom or bedroom without knocking and receiving permission to enter.

19. All family members will be dressed at all times (pajamas or robes are OK if covering adequately).

20. Alcohol and drug use is completely and strictly prohibited if substance use was in any way involved in previous sex offenses.

21. For offenders who have not used alcohol or drugs in previous offenses, rules for moderate use will be established.

22. No pornography or sexually oriented material (magazines, pictures, or videos) will be in the home..

(Reprinted with permission from *Connections Workbook*, Sage Publications, Inc., October 2000.)

In my experience of working with sex offenders, I have developed some boundaries that sex offenders should not cross that will reduce their risk to re-offend or prevent others from committing a first sexual offense. After listing these boundaries, I will discuss concerns I have about several of Levenson and Morin's boundaries and elaborate on case examples of sex offenders crossing these boundaries to commit their sex crime. The following boundaries also apply to anyone accused of a sex offense.

1. No children are to sit in a sex offender's lap.

2. No children are to sit beside a sex offender with cover over their bodies.

3. Sex offenders will not swim with children; it is too easy to touch inappropriately.

4. Sex offenders are not allowed to take pictures or videos of children without an adult present who is aware of their sex offense.

5. Sex offenders are not allowed to examine a child's body for any concerns (bruises, scratches).

6. Sex offenders are not allowed to have children in their car without another adult who is aware of their sex offense.

7. Sex offenders cannot congregate where children are or be in an authority role relative to the children.

8. No alcohol is to be given to anyone under 18.

9. No Internet use is allowed if the Internet was used in the sex offense. Otherwise, no pornographic sites are to be accessed.

10. No adults will sleep with children under the age of 18.

11. Physical affection between a sex offender and anyone under the age of 18 will be by a brief arm hug around the shoulder, no face-to-face hugging, and in the presence of another adult who is aware of the previous sexual misconduct.

12. The offender will keep all scheduled appointments and take pre-
    scribed medications if referred to a psychiatrist.

13. Sex offenders will not have children's toys or video games that are
    intended for children. These can be used as lures for children.

Even though these boundaries were initially developed for sex offenders, they
are safe boundaries for family members to follow in order to prevent allegations of sexual misconduct and provide protection for children. Sexual assault
is an issue of power, control, and boundaries. It is more difficult to commit
sexual offenses if safe boundaries are respected at all times. The problem lies in
individuals not knowing the difference between safe and risky boundaries.
Boundaries cannot be stressed enough in order to prevent sexual misconduct
from occurring or an accusation being made. Paying attention to behaviors is a
key to preventing sexual abuse and protecting children. Another problem in
prevention is that individuals who commit such crimes frequently appear to be
trustworthy, which makes it even more difficult to develop safe boundaries.
Many sex offenders operate by being helpful to others in stressful times. They
may play the role of a father figure or do some work for the family members in
order to gain more access to the children. They may have other children over
to be around their child so they can gradually commit their offense. Rapists
may initially help out their victims in a needful time and then rape them right
afterward or come back later and rape them. All of these behaviors make it
appear that the person is being good, but they can actually be used to set up an
opportunity to cross a sexual boundary. Many of the aforementioned boundaries are frequently practiced in most homes and seem appropriate. To prevent
and protect, each household must clarify what the boundaries are to keep children safe in their home. These guidelines can be altered as needed.

I will now discuss the boundaries that were developed by Levenson and
Morin. Based on my experience of providing group treatment to sex offenders
and recognizing their grooming behaviors, I have questions about some of
Levenson and Morin's boundaries. I appreciate the boundaries they have
developed regarding re-unification with a sex offender. However, I tell sex
offenders that there are certain privileges they do not have any longer since
they have committed a sex offense.

Their boundary number eight is confusing to me. It states, "Physical affection between offender and children will be brief and will avoid bodily contact."

How does one have physical affection without bodily contact? The boundary (number eleven) I developed is even questionable. It states, "Physical affection between a sex offender and children will be by a brief arm hug around the shoulder, no face-to-face hugging, and in the presence of another adult." In one of my group treatment sessions, one sex offender, Steve, reached over to another sex offender to demonstrate this boundary. His behavior was inappropriate the way Steve touched the other group member. Steve put one arm around the back of the other person on the shoulder area and his other arm around the front of the person across the breast area but was touching the shoulder area. Had he not done this, I would have taken for granted that this boundary was understood. His behavior was inappropriate even though he thought he was being appropriate. The arm cannot go around the front of the minor and touch the breast area. He was not face-to-face, but side-to-side. Only shoulder areas can be touching and no other parts of the body.

I am concerned about number eighteen of Levenson and Morin's boundaries. Number eighteen states, "No family member shall enter a bathroom or bedroom without knocking and receiving permission to enter." I am unclear if number eighteen includes the sex offender. Sex offenders should not be allowed to enter a child's bedroom or bathroom under any circumstances, even if permission is given by a child or adult.

Several sex offenders I have treated were convicted due to inappropriate sexual behavior in the bathroom. Jim admits allowing his four- and five-year-old daughters to come into the bathroom and see him naked, and one of his children said he had a tail. The allegations were much more severe than this. Whatever the manner in which his children were sexually violated, had there been no contact in the bathroom or bedroom, the risk of these children being sexually violated could have been reduced, as well as the risk of him being accused. Another sex offender, Harry, took showers with his four-year-old nephew and masturbated to pornography in the bedroom in front of his nephew. It is not a child's responsibility to set limits around bathrooms and bedrooms. Another sex offender had been sleeping nude in the bed with his wife and her child, his third victim. They thought it was acceptable.

I also have a concern about Levenson and Morin's boundary number fifteen. "If mutually agreed, children will be permitted to lock doors." I worked with a mother, Martha, and her two daughters, Laura and June. Her oldest daughter Laura was sexually abused at age eleven by her husband, Laura's stepfather. Laura had never met her father. Laura's stepfather had been violent toward her mother. He took the lock off the bathroom door and took Laura's door off her bedroom. Laura described instances in which he would come into the bathroom. Martha had separated from this sex offender and had let him back in the home against child protective services' orders and had told Laura not to tell anyone. Laura eventually told the school counselor. At the time I worked with them, Martha still had not put a lock on the bathroom door. What a trigger of sexual abuse it was for this child to have no lock to use in the bathroom. We went over boundaries, and Laura was very happy to know that no other man could discipline her or set rules about her locking her door. It is not recommended sex offenders make the decision whether a child locks the bathroom or bedroom door. Unlocked doors give sex offenders easy access.

Before discussing some more case examples, I will discuss the reactions of sex offenders, their spouses, and significant others regarding these boundaries. It is likely many of these boundaries seem normal in families. These are accepted behaviors in most homes; however, you are being challenged to pay very close attention to behavior. Thus, crossing these boundaries and others I may not have listed is how many sex offenses are committed. If household members would seriously take a look at the risk in their behaviors, sex offenses could be reduced. In my treatment of sex offenders, I have seen that wives and others are the most resistant to following these boundaries. They think the boundaries are absurd. One thirty-eight-year-old male victim I worked with had been sexually abused by his stepmother when he was sixteen for a period of six months. He had confronted his stepmother by letter, and then the three of us had a session together. She presented as most sex offenders do, blaming the victim, justifying her behavior, pleading with her victim not to tell her husband, his father. She wanted her victim to participate in keeping her secret. She ignored the impact on her victim and took on the victim's role. He saw the boundaries to keep his children safe as punishment. These boundaries are not punishment—they are protection. This woman was an unconvicted, untreated female sex offender. The fact is that there are more untreated, unconvicted sex offenders in society than convicted and treated sex offenders. However, people generally become enraged at known sex offenders rather than focusing on educating themselves about what to look for to prevent sexually inappropriate behavior. People fail to recognize risky behavior that could be a setup to commit a sex crime with children. A sex offense pattern begins long before the actual act. Being able to recognize risky behaviors of adults around children is a crucial key to preventing sexual assault. Some people believe a myth that people in particular occupations or wealthy people would not sexually abuse children. One lady I worked with could not believe that her husband, a pilot, would have sexually offended their two boys, as they alleged he did. She did not believe he was capable of such a crime because he was an upstanding man. Occupation and status are not exemptions to committing sex offenses. The reality is that no type or category of individual is incapable of a sexual offense.

Now I will give case examples of specific boundaries that sex offenders cross in order to sexually violate. Levenson and Morin state in number sixteen, "All family members will sleep in their own beds." This is important for juveniles as well as adults. In many states, there can be a potential charge for a sex offense if there is a three-year age difference For instance sexual contact by a 12-year-old towards a 9-year-old could result in a criminal sexual charge. There are many juvenile sex offenders. Sleeping arrangements are very important, and much attention needs to be given to children sleeping with children, as well as any adults sleeping with children, to prevent sexual misconduct.

The following is an example of how a sex offender disclosed that the family members were not sleeping in their own beds and then attempted to justify the sleeping arrangements. I did a pre-sentence sex offender evaluation with a twenty-eight-year-old mentally challenged female who planned on pleading guilty to sexual misconduct towards a ten-year-old female. During my assessment, the woman disclosed some information about sleeping arrangements in her household. Her own nine-year-old male child, had, since birth, always slept with an adult woman named Sarah with whom the mother had lived since her own birth. This was an inappropriate sleeping arrangement and, therefore, constituted a risk for Sarah. The nine-year-old could have accused Sarah of sexually inappropriate behavior. This child was nearing an age to be sexually curious and should not have been sleeping with an adult female. Moreover, who is to say that Sarah had not already been sexually inappropriate towards him? The two women tried to justify this child sleeping with an adult female by saying that it was the only place he had to sleep and that his mother could not wake up as needed to his crying when he was a baby. He was no longer a baby, and they could have made other arrangements.

It should also be noted that there are many incidents of sibling sexual abuse, which is another reason to pay strict attention to sleeping arrangements in households. Because juvenile sex offense cases are sealed, it is more difficult to identify incidences of sibling sexual abuse. However, juveniles are also treated in group settings. Many of them are also in residential settings. My colleague and I have treated adults who began committing sex offenses as juveniles. I have worked with victims who were sexually abused by siblings, as well as offenders who sexually assaulted their siblings. To learn more about sibling sexual abuse, I recommend Vernon Wiehe's book *Brother Sister Hurt.*

Levenson and Morin state in number twelve, "Offender will never enter the children's bedroom alone." From my experience, offenders should not enter children's bedrooms ever, but especially alone. Offenders should never place themselves in any situation where they can be accused of offending or have an opportunity to offend. Offenders can begin to sexually fantasize by having knowledge of the bedroom or materials in the bedroom. Deviant thinking can begin. One offender knew some children would go to the bedroom and play. In his mind, he believed the children were in there having sex. No one can read minds; therefore, all safety measures must be taken. Offenders begin to plan ways to act on whatever fantasy they may be having in their head. How does one detect fantasies?

Levenson and Morin state in number five, "Offender will never be responsible for babysitting or supervising children." This is a good safety plan to follow. Many sex offenses are committed while babysitting. It puts the sex offender in a position of authority and power over the victim. The victim is told by the parents to do whatever the babysitter says. Sex offenders disguised as helpers by babysitting thereby gain easy access to sexually abuse children.

Number six by Levenson and Morin states, "Discipline of the children will be done primarily by the non-offending caretaker." Using the word *primarily* implies that the sex offender may sometimes exercise discipline. Sex offenders may use discipline as a way to manipulate children. They will not discipline them as severely as the other children in exchange for sexually abusing them. Sometimes they will threaten to discipline them more. This is a privilege that sex offenders should not have once they have sexually offended. Granted, mothers and other caretakers get tired and irritable and just want some help in the discipline area. Nevertheless, it is extremely important for mothers to pay attention to how discipline might be being used inappropriately, or prohibit discipline if they are living with a convicted or accused sex offender.

Levenson and Morin state in number seven, "Offender will not discuss sex or dating with the children." Numerous sex offenders will provide a listening ear for young girls who have questions about sexuality. Children sometimes discuss their age appropriate sexual activity with adults. One grandfather my colleague and I treated would listen to his granddaughter talk about sex with her boyfriend when she was using the telephone while at his house. Instead of instructing his granddaughter that she should go elsewhere to talk about these matters with her boyfriend, he continued listening to her conversations and became sexually interested in her even though he was impotent. Some people believe it is necessary to have an erection to commit a sex offense. It is not necessary to have a penis or an erection to commit a sex offense. His sexual conversations with her can be considered a sexual offense. Sexual conversations can lead to hands on sex offenses as in this case. Discussing dating with children can be appropriate or made inappropriate by a sex offender or potential sex offender. Sex offenders may listen to children discuss dating and sexual activity, and then tell themselves that it is acceptable for them to be sexual with these children because the children are already sexually active. Conversely, someone who does not choose to sexually offend will direct the minor to an appropriate person for guidance regarding his or her behavior.

Levenson and Morin state in number ten, "There will be no tickling or wrestling between offender and children." My colleague and I treated one sex offender who swore that all he did was tickle his victim. We questioned how one got himself ordered by the court to obtain sex offender treatment for tickling and pointed out that there was no law against tickling. Many sex offenders in treatment admit to grooming their victim by tickling and wrestling with them before touching them sexually. It is a way for a sex offender to pretend he is accidentally touching private areas, and he pays attention to the reaction of the minor to determine how much further he can sexually act out.

Levenson and Morin state in number nineteen, "All family members will be dressed at all times (pajamas or robes are OK if covering adequately)." Sex offenders look at children who are dressed in T-shirts and panties as flirting with them. They will sexualize the child's behavior. Some sex offenders will intentionally dress in clothing that allows their penises to be seen, and then act as though they didn't realize their penis was hanging out. I treated an offender who had been exposing himself since he was a teen. He would wear extremely short shorts and then pretend that his penis accidentally slipped out of his shorts.

Levenson and Morin state in number twenty, "Alcohol and drug use is completely and strictly prohibited if substance use was in any way involved in previous sex offenses." In a significant number of the sex offenses that are committed, alcohol or drugs played a role. In the boundary that I set in number eight it states, "No alcohol is to be given to anyone under eighteen." Alcohol and other drugs are frequently given to victims by sex offenders. In my opinion, if one has committed a sex offense, one should not use alcohol or drugs at all.

Levenson and Morin state in number twenty-two, "No pornography or sexually oriented material (magazines, pictures, or videos) will be in the home." Sex offenders oftentimes introduce victims to pornography to observe their reaction and desensitize them to what they may be preparing to do to the victim. Even sex offenders who have been convicted and are on probation will keep pornography. It is a violation of probation to have any type of pornography while on probation and can result in one's probation being revoked. Pornography is unacceptable if one has committed a sex offense.

I will now give some examples of sex offenders committing their crime by crossing boundaries I devised. Number one states, "No children are to sit in a sex offender's lap." Many sex offenders groom their victims and begin their sexual fantasy and planning from a child sitting in their lap. They become sexually aroused and ignore the child's age. Children like affection and will jump into people's laps. If someone has never been convicted of a sex offense, it will be difficult to determine whether that person is engaging in sexually inappropriate behavior. It is behavior that needs close attention to when a child is sitting on an adult's lap. If the person has been convicted of a sex offense, that person cannot under any circumstances be permitted to have a child on his lap. If he or she will not take responsibility and refuse to engage in this behavior, then some other adult will have to take on that responsibility and not allow that person having children on his or her lap.

Number four states, "Sex offenders are not allowed to take pictures or videos of children without an adult present who is aware of their sex offense." I did an assessment of a sex offender who was ordered by the court to undertake treatment. This was his account: He was out in public on the side of the road taking pictures of two teen girls who were fully clothed. He was taking these pictures for another person to put in her scrapbook. He stated that one of the girls' mother's friends rode by and saw him taking the pictures. She went and told the mother. The mother went to his house demanding the pictures. Why was there a problem here? This man had not been convicted of anything. He had no criminal record. The problem was that this man had created suspicion about his behavior and then was resistant when the police officer contacted him to discuss the pictures he had taken. Due to his attitude, a search warrant was obtained, which resulted in evidence of criminal sexual conduct on his part: Child pornography was found on his computer.

Other sex offenders take pictures of their victims in the nude. One sex offender took pictures of his victim's breast area. Another sex offender who was seventy years old videotaped two teens in the nude and kept the video.

This constituted good evidence to get him convicted. I have had training from Robert Farley. He is an undercover officer in Chicago who arrests people who are attempting sexual crimes through the Internet. Some of the material that he has collected is overwhelming. He had confiscated video material where a man and woman were out in public for more than eight hours videotaping people's bodies, such as their leg areas, and staking out what child they wanted to molest. Household members need to pay close attention to who is taking pictures and videotaping.

Number five states, "Sex offenders are not allowed to examine a child's body for any concerns (bruises, scratches)." One sex offender committed his offense in the state of Florida and received fifteen years of probation. He had not had any sex offender group treatment upon conviction. He sexually offended his twin daughters when they were approximately age seven. He and his wife had a conflictive divorce. He remarried and had another child. Twelve years later, he was having visitation with his daughters, and one of his daughters complained of chest pain, claiming that her brother had been kicking her in this area. He did not believe in doctors, and the Department of Social Services had previously cited him for neglect when he did not take one of his children to the doctor for proper care. He decided to examine his prior victim's breast area for any bruising. This was a risk situation for him, and thus inappropriate. He was eventually charged with a sex crime again. At that point, his probation officer ordered him to sex offender group treatment. When he began treatment, he wanted to blame his ex-wife, did not think he had done anything inappropriate, and thought he was being a good father for examining his daughter's breast area. He is fortunate that he was acquitted of this behavior. Does an acquittal mean that he was not guilty of inappropriate behavior? No, it just means he was not criminally liable. In treatment, risky situations are discussed frequently. Not having had group treatment, he did not recognize his behavior as risky even though it would seem like common sense.

Number six states, "Sex offenders are not allowed to have children in their car without another adult who is aware of their sex offense." Significant others need to pay attention when adults are riding in the car with minors. One sex offender, Jeff, was teaching his stepdaughter, Erin, to drive and would touch her breast while allowing her to drive. This is sexually violating by exchanging privileges for sexual favors. This sex offender's wife, Jane, had refused to get her own license, so Jeff had to do all the driving for their large family. Jeff would act angry toward Jane's father, who had sexually abused Jane while they were swimming when she was a child. Jane would tell herself she was being paranoid when she was having suspicions that Jeff might be behaving sexually inappropriately towards her daughter. Jane also did not believe Jeff would sexually offend because of his reaction toward her father. On Anna Salter's video, *Truth, Lies, and Sex Offenders,* one of the sex offenders she interviewed admitted being in the back seat of the car with a male child who he was molesting while his parents were in the front seat. This is called not paying attention. This is also how sly sex offenders are.

Number seven states, "Sex offenders cannot congregate where children are or be in an authority role relative to the children." Many sex offenders are churchgoers. They are in positions of authority over children, especially youth activities. Sex offenders know church members are too trusting, making it easy to deceive fellow church members. The Catholic Church is a prime example in light of the cover-up by the church about ministers molesting children. Scout leaders are also people in positions of authority over children. The problem is that, if an individual has never been convicted of a sex offense, criminal behavior is difficult to detect. Sex offenders are also good at playing children's games in order to reduce the defenses of minors. Children love attention. Society has to make it safer for children to disclose in order for the problem to be further reduced.

7

The Effects of Sexual Assault

This book is entitled *Impact* in reference to the devastating effects of sexual assault on everyone involved. As professionals, therapists can attempt to help survivors identify how they were impacted and challenge sex offenders to identify how they impacted and, more specifically, harmed their victims. Significant Others are also impacted in their own ways. However, is it genuinely possible to comprehend the impact of having been sexually assaulted? Even though many survivors heal, become successful, and move on with their lives, the sexual violation may still manifest itself at unwanted times. No matter how much survivors try to forget or block out the events, a trigger may get activated that can remind them of what happened. How can the impact of sexual assault be measured? Impact is an internal process that is difficult to observe. We try to measure the impact on different individuals based on their mental health, stability, relationships, success, social skills, and self-reporting. I will address some areas in which many survivors are impacted. What follows applies mostly to adults; because children are still developing, they are unlikely to recognize the impact fully until they have reached adulthood.

An issue affecting the impact of abuse is the need of empathy for victims. Part of the treatment for sex offenders is to try and give them some sense of empathy for the victim, which is not the same as sympathy. This is one of the most difficult areas of treatment for sex offenders to make progress in. When they achieve empathy with their victims, that is, they can put themselves in their victim's shoes and try to feel what their victim felt if the same thing had been done to them, then (if they can retain that empathy) their risk of reoffending could possibly be reduced. One sex offender had been a policeman for fifteen years and stated that he had harmed his community. As part of his plea bargain, he had to move away from his community. I believe that is an indication that they are benefiting from the treatment when sex offenders acknowledge ways in which they have harmed others that the therapist had not thought of. Another offender, John, who had been in treatment in another county before entering our program was asked what he addressed in treatment, his response was that the members of his treatment group did not talk about the offense, but mostly about their own self-esteem instead. It is recommended that all sex offenders in treatment address how they impacted and more specifically harmed their victim.

In the following descriptions, the instances of negative effects resulting from the impact of sexual assault may be constant or occasional. Survivors choose how they will cope with having been sexually assaulted. Some allow it to ruin their lives, others choose to ignore it; and still others choose to resolve it, heal, and move on. Resolution of each of the problem areas listed below is a step in the healing process.

• <u>Affecting the sense of safety.</u> When victims are sexually violated in their homes, their homes no longer give them a sense of safety. If they were violated elsewhere, the world no longer feels safe. One sex offender I treated pulled a knife on a teenage girl as he was walking her home. He had groomed her to trust him by waiting for her at the bus stop and walking her back to her house. He had planned to rape her, but did not follow through when he saw the look on her face. Does this survivor feel safe or is she wondering who will pull a knife on her next? This victim moved, and the community cut down the trees in the area where the sex offender lived. Obviously neither she nor the community felt safe near him. He was confronted with harming her by robbing her of her sense of safety. For this survivor, regaining a sense of safety will be a step forward in the healing process.

• <u>Interfering with emotional well-being.</u> Survivors experience shame, guilt, anger, and other emotions. Survivors carry the offenders' shame and guilt without realizing that they are doing so. The difference between shame and guilt is that when survivors feel shame they believe there is something wrong with them. When they feel guilt they believe that they did something wrong. Both shame and guilt have to be given to the sex offenders to increase healing.

<u>Shame</u>	<u>Guilt</u>
There's something wrong with me	I did something wrong
You're being (who you are)	Behavior

Survivors must get to a point where they can do a cognitive switch and begin saying to themselves, "There was nothing wrong with me; there was something wrong with him. I did nothing wrong; he did something wrong." The tendency to self-blame may be intensified among those survivors who arranged a meeting with whomever through the Internet or any other means. Arranging to meet someone is not a license to sexually violate, as one of my survivors said. These negative emotions about the self lead to a lack of confidence. Before sex offenders sexually violate, they often have negative emotions about themselves, while survivors begin to harbor negative emotions about themselves after the sexual assault. Resolving the negative emotions about the self is another step in the healing process.

•<u>Developing distorted thinking.</u> Survivors' ability to see clearly is clouded by irrational thoughts that lead to misinterpretation of information. A large percentage of persons who have been sexually abused are now adults and have never been able to talk about their sexual abuse in a non-threatening atmosphere. A contemporary example is the number of adult men who were sexually abused as boys by priests in the Catholic Church. Because survivors could not clarify what was being done to them at the time they were sexually violated, they have difficulty clarifying information in the present. A seven-year-old girl I worked with, Pat, had been sexually violated at age four by the eleven-year-old boy who lived next door. Her mother had told her that they moved from that house because of him. The parents were paying two mortgages and fought a good deal. Pat would hear them arguing about the house payments. She told me they moved from that house because of the highway. How long will Pat choose to believe they moved because of the highway? Survivors have to challenge the beliefs they developed as a result of the sexual violation to aid their healing process.

•<u>Destroying the ability to trust.</u> When survivors are sexually violated, they are betrayed. As a result, survivors sometimes come to expect that everyone will eventually betray them: spouses, parents, children, friends, and coworkers. This destruction of trust is enhanced when survivors were not initially believed or were blamed. For survivors, learning to trust others can be a lifetime struggle. Beginning to trust others increases the survivor's healing.

•<u>Failing to recognize the ability to exert control</u>. The general public believes that sex offenses are about sex. Professionals know that sex offenses are generally about power and control issues that are acted out in a sexual manner. When people are sexually violated, they have no power or control, and therefore survivors fail to recognize the control that they do have in their lives. They falsely believe they cannot accomplish many goals to which they would otherwise aspire. They regularly feel controlled by others, but lack the skills to be assertive under such circumstances. They tend to interpret others as controlling them when others may actually be trying to help them. This is often the case between many survivors and their spouses. Couples, in particular, have to work out their control issues. For example, consider the case of Patricia, who, as an adult, pressed charges against her offender. (He was charged with sexually violating four victims and is currently serving a life sentence.) Patricia now admits that she is a control freak. She has to control everything in the life of her two-year-old child and will not allow the child to visit her husband's sister's house. She still holds her mother accountable for her having been sexually abused. Her husband's sister reminds her too much of her mother, and she fears her daughter may be sexually abused if allowed to visit. She and her husband argue back and forth. Until a sense of trust can be restored to Patricia, there will be no visitation.

•Developing a poor body image. Survivors may feel uncomfortable with their bodies and with their own sexuality, and view sex as something dirty and unclean. Some survivors cope by becoming anorexic, while others may gain excessive weight. They do not enjoy sex with their husband or sexual partner, but pretend to do so to maintain the relationship. They are unable to discuss their true feelings about sex with their sexual partner. Survivors will know they are healing when they reach a point of being comfortable with their own body and sexuality.

•Becoming suicidal. Survivors may see themselves as useless, worthless, less than everyone else, unworthy, unwanted, or misunderstood, yet fail to understand that these feelings have developed as a result of someone else's behavior, not their own behavior. When survivors continue to put themselves down with negative self-talk, they continue to give the sex offender power over them. Some reach the point of believing that death is better than these feelings. Unfortunately, many survivors continue to batter themselves emotionally long after the sexual assault. Survivors are the only ones who have the power to begin making healthy statements about themselves to themselves. This is an internal process that will bring about healing.

•Impaired coping skills. Some survivors' ability to cope with everyday life situations becomes impaired for extended periods following a sexual assault. They have a tendency to "awfulize." They see the worst thing that can happen and do not see situations on a continuum of possible worst, best, and neutral outcomes of a problem. Most of the time, neither the worst or best thing happens, but something in the middle. When survivors are able to recognize best, worst, or neutral outcomes of situations, they will know they are healing and that their coping skills are improving.

•Developing Dissociative Identity Disorder. Survivors who were sexually violated in a manner whereby their sex organs were penetrated with objects or at
an early age for an extended period sometimes develop Dissociative Identity
Disorder (previously known as Multiple Personality Disorder). According to
the DSM-IV, it is diagnosed three to nine times more frequently in adult
females than in adult males. Symptoms include having two or more distinct
identities, each with its own pattern of perceiving, relating to, or thinking
about itself or its environment. These survivors have severe difficulty function-
ing in everyday life. There is an inability to recall significant personal information when one of the identities takes control of the person's behavior.
Different personalities address different aspects of the abuse. Therapy can take
as long as seven years or more. By contrast, few sex offenders spend ten years
in treatment. When survivors suffering from Dissociative Identity Disorder
stop splitting into multiple personalities in order to cope with having been
sexually violated, healing is taking place.

•Feeling undeserving. Survivors may not believe they deserve many things in
life. Something good may happen to them, and they try to enjoy it, but doing
so is a struggle because they see themselves as damaged. They say things to
themselves like, "If people only knew, they would not do this for me." Survivors will know they are healing when they allow themselves to deserve good
things.

•Experiencing negative emotions. At some point most survivors will experience one or more of the following: depression, anxiety, sadness, grief, post-
traumatic stress, low self-esteem, and other negative emotions. Survivors are
so used to thinking that the way they are feeling is abnormal or that they are
abnormal that they miss how normal they are. Once survivors begin to recognize their normalcy, another step in the healing process has occurred.

Ironically, many of the ways in which survivors are impacted resemble the
emotional problems that sex offenders are already experiencing before they
sexually violate. Sex offenders definitely have control and power issues. They
have to use distorted thinking in order to sexually violate. They are suicidal at
times. They have poor coping skills and negative emotions, and they do not
trust others. It is sad that they usually do not address these issues until after
they have been convicted of sexually violating and are in a treatment program.

Some survivors never move beyond the impact of having been sexually violated and never learn to manage their lives in a healthy way. The depth of the impact of sexual violations is difficult to comprehend and describe. Many survivors have put much energy into keeping the impact unknown. I am sure there are survivors who could tell me I had missed some ways in which they were impacted by a sexual violation. All survivors need to identify how they were impacted and then find their own ways of healing. The above list represents some of the ways in which victims are impacted. No one can list all the specific ways victims are impacted, but each victim has to identify how he or she was impacted. The aforementioned list can jump-start the process.

All sex offenders need to identify their offense patterns, grooming behaviors, thinking errors, risk situations, and ways to prevent themselves from re-offending. All significant others, mothers, or other caretakers need to identify signs they missed and identify ways to protect children in every way possible. It is possible for the impact of sexual assault to be reduced by the way family members, significant others, the general public, and the legal system respond to sexual violations. Healing is a lifelong process and continues in various ways throughout life. Regardless of the age of the victims when they were sexually assaulted, they can always resolve what happened to them. In some manner, the sexual violations will raise their ugly heads. Each time a memory of sexual violations comes, it is an opportunity to further heal. Victims tend to wish they could stop thinking about what happened to them. They do temporarily, but then a reminder comes. Go with those reminders and look at what needs to be healed at the present time.

This book has provided the information needed to examine thinking errors regarding sex offenses. Examples were given of thinking errors, as well as corrected thinking, for sex offenders, victims, and significant others. Most people have power over their thinking, which can help prevent sexual assaults. The more you correct your thinking, the safer children will become.

Factors were given that influence the impact of sexual assault. Providing support can reduce the impact. Not blaming victims and painting them as emotionally unstable can help reduce the impact. In addition, similarities between victims and offenders were demonstrated. Being able to point out to victims that they are thinking or behaving like offenders can provoke them to move forward and change their thoughts to begin to feel better about themselves. On the other hand, calling offenders on their attitudes towards victims can provoke them to move forward and take responsibility for their behavior.

Specific treatment steps were given for offenders, victims, and significant others. If all persons involved get appropriate treatment, further sex offenses will be reduced. Sex offenses are not a single-population issue.

There was a discussion of safe boundaries that each household member can practice to prevent sexual assaults. These safe behaviors cannot be stressed enough.

This book has provided enough information to identify significant thoughts, behaviors, and feelings—currently or previously ignored—that would lead to the prevention of a sexual crime. As the book cover implies, if the people on the railroad track ignore the train, they are going to be impacted. However, if they recognize the danger coming, they can prevent a disaster, as you can if you apply the information you have gained from this book.

Appendices

Types of Sex Offenses

Hands off/sex offenses

Indecent exposure

Looking in a sexual manner

Making obscene telephone calls

Allowing a child to witness sexual behavior

Having sexual conversation

Showing pornography/making pornographic videos

Hands on/sex offenses

Fondling

Touching sexual organs

Making a child touch sex organs

Attempted/actual intercourse

Forcing or coercing sexual contact

Non-Sex Offender Behavior

What would a sex offender, mother, other caretaker, or survivor look for to know a sex offender had changed? If a sex offender has changed, one could expect to see the following behavioral changes.

SEX OFFENDER BEHAVIOR	BEHAVIORAL CHANGES
Keeps secrets	Opens up and reveals information
Irresponsible in everyday living	Responsible in everyday living
Denies	Admits
Blames victim, others, drugs	Focuses responsibility on self, not others
Indirect, evasive, withholds information	Direct, answers questions
Lies	Is truthful, forthcoming
Avoids treatment, and addressing problems	Addresses problems, attends treatment
Manipulates	Takes advice
Plays the victim role	Does not behave as a victim
Feels sorry for self, has pity parties	Admits he or she is the problem
Story makes no sense	Story makes sense
Won't maintain a job	Will keep a job
Won't meet financial obligations	Financially responsible

Positive Emotions

After a sexual assault, victims have difficulty feeling positive emotions. Before a sex offense, offenders often don't have positive emotions. The goal is for offenders to have appropriate, positive emotions so they don't re-offend, and for victims to regain positive emotions after a sexual assault. The following list gives examples of words that can be used to describe positive emotions.

Accepted	Dedicated	Grateful	Peaceful
Adequate	Delighted	Great	Pleased
Adored	Desirable	Happy	Powerful
Admired	Determined	Healthy	Proud
Assured	Devoted	Helpful	Protected
Beautiful	Eager	Hopeful	Relaxed
Brave	Ecstatic	Included	Respected
Calm	Elated	Important	Responsible
Capable	Empowered	Interested	Safe
Certain	Enthusiastic	Inspired	Satisfied
Cheerful	Fantastic	Joyful	Secure
Comfortable	Fine	Lovable	Self-reliant
Competent	Fulfilled	Magnificent	Sexy
Confident	Generous	Marvelous	Special
Content	Glad	Motivated	Strong
Courageous	Good	Optimistic	Supported
Curious	Gratified	Overjoyed	Sure

Positive Emotions (Contd.)

Terrific

Thankful

Thrilled

Uplifted

Understood

Valuable

Warm

Wise

Wonderful

Worthwhile

Negative Emotions

For victims, focusing too much on negative emotions sets them up for depression and anxiety. For offenders, it could be a set-up for a re-offense. Recognizing that they are focusing on the negative is critical to helping bring them emotional stability by looking at the positive. The following list gives examples of words that can be used to describe negative emotions.

Abandoned	Bored	Disempowered	Forsaken
Afraid	Bothered	Disgraced	Fragile
Aggravated	Burned	Disgusted	Frightened
Agitated	Callous	Disliked	Frustrated
Alarmed	Confused	Disrespected	Furious
Alienated	Criticized	Distressed	Gloomy
Alone	Crushed	Disturbed	Grief
Angry	Deceived	Dread	Guilty
Annoyed	Defeated	Dumb	Helpless
Anxious	Degraded	Embarrassed	Hopeless
Apprehensive	Desperate	Empty	Horrified
Ashamed	Despairing	Enraged	Hostile
Awful	Despised	Excluded	Humiliated
Awkward	Destroyed	Envious	Hurt
Bashful	Devalued	Exposed	Ignored
Belittled	Devalued	Fear	Impaired
Betrayed	Devastated	Feeble	Imprisoned
Blamed	Disappointed	Fidgety	Inadequate
Blue	Discounted	Foolish	Incapable

Negative Emotions (Contd.)

Incompetent	Mocked	Put Down	Troubled
Indecisive	Nauseated	Rebellious	Unable
Inept	Needy	Regret	Unaccepted
Inferior	Neglected	Rejected	Unappreciated
Inhibited	Nervous	Remorse	Unattractive
Insignificant	Numb	Revengeful	Uncertain
Insecure	Odd	Resentful	Uncomfortable
Insensitive	Offended	Reprimanded	Underestimated
Intimidated	On Edge	Restless	Uneasy
Irritated	Oppressed	Restricted	Unfulfilled
Isolated	Ostracized	Ridiculed	Unhappy
Jealous	Outraged	Ridiculous	Unimportant
Jittery	Overwhelmed	Rotten	Unloved
Left Out	Panicky	Sad	Unsure
Lonely	Paralyzed	Stupid	Used
Lost	Perplexed	Superior	Useless
Lousy	Perturbed	Suspicious	Uptight
Low	Pessimistic	Terrified	Violated
Mad	Powerless	Threatened	Vulnerable
Miserable	Pressured	Tired	Weird
Misunderstood	Provoked	Trapped	Weak

Negative Emotions (Contd.)

Shamed

Shy

Skeptical

Sorrow

Speechless

Stuck

Weary

Worn Out

Worried

Worthless

Scared

Self-conscious

Recommended Readings

For Survivors

The Invisible Wound	Wayne Kristberg
Toxic Parents	Susan Forward
Memory and Abuse	Charles Whitfield
Sexual Violence: Our War Against Rape	Linda Fairstein
Recovering from Rape	Linda Ledray
The Brother–Sister Hurt	Vernon Wiehe
Sexual Healing Journey	Wendy Maltz
Sexual Anorexia: Overcoming Sexual Self-Hatred	Patrick Carnes
The Magic of Sex/(Healthy Sexuality)	Miriam Stoppard
The Assertiveness Workbook	Randy Paterson
Anger Free	Doyle Gentry
Letting Go of Anger	Ron Potter-Effron
Don't Divorce Us	Rita Sommers-Flannagan

For Significant Others

Ghosts in the Bedroom	Ken Graber
Outgrowing the Pain Together	Eliana Gil
When Your Child Has Been Molested	Kathryn Hagan

For Mothers, Caretakers, and Sex Offenders

Connections Workbook	Jill Levenson and John Morin
The Adult Relapse Prevention Workbook	Charlene Steen

For Professionals

Transforming Trauma	Anna Salter
Systemic Treatment of Families Who Abuse	Eliana Gil
Sexualized Children: Children Who Molest	Gil, & Toni Cavanaugh
Psychotherapy with Sexually Abused Boys	William Friedrich
Psychotherapy with Abused Children and Their Families	William Friedrich
The Invisible Wound	Wayne Kristberg
Abused Boys	Mic Hunter
The Healing Power of Play	Eliana Gil
Understanding Your Child's Sexual Behavior	Toni Cavanaugh
Treating Abused Adolescents	Eliana Gil
Trauma and Recovery	Judith Herman
Women Who Hurt Themselves	Dusty Miller
Men Who Rape	Nicholos Groth
Supervision of the Sex Offender	Cumming & Bell
Treating Child Sex Offenders and Victims	Anna Salter
Cognitive Behavioral Therapy with Sex Offenders	William Marshall
Relapse Prevention with Sex Offenders	Richard Laws
Sexual Violence: Our War Against Rape	Linda Fairstein

Bibliography

Bussiere, M. T., and Bussiere, M. K., & K.Hanson (1998). "Predicting relapse: A meta-analysis of sexual offender recidivism studies." *Journal of Consulting and Clinical Psychology* 66(2): 348–362.

Carnes, P. (1997). *Sexual Anoxeria:Overcoming Sexual Self-hatred.*. Minnesota. Hazeldon Information & Educational Services.

Cumming, G., and Buell,(1997). *Supervision of the Sex Offender*. Vermont. Safer Society.

Fairstein, L. (1995). *Sexual Violence: Our War Against Rape*. New York. William Morrow & Col, Inc.

Forward, S. & Buck, C. (2002). *Toxic Parents*. New York. Bantam Doubleday Dell Publishing.

Friedrich, W. (1995). *Psychotherapy with Sexually Abused Boys*. California. Sage Publications.

Friedrich, W. (1990). *Psychotherapy with Abused Children and Their Families*. California. Sage Publications.

Gentry, D. (2000). *Anger Free*. New York. Harper Collins Publisher.

Gil, E. & Cavanaugh-Johnson, T. (1993). *Sexualized Children: Children Who Molest*. United States. Launch Press.

Gil, E. (1996). *Treating Abused Adolescents*. New York. Guilford Publications.

Gil, E. (1995). *Systemic Treatment of Families Who Abuse*. California. Jossey-Bass, Inc.

Gil, E. (1992). *Outgrowing the Pain Together*. Dell Publishing, Inc.

Gil, E. (1991). *The Healing Power of Play*. New York. Guilford Publications.

Graber, K. (1991). *Ghosts in the Bedroom*. Florida. Health Communications, Inc.

Groth, N. (1979). *Men Who Rape*. New York. Plenum Press.

Hagan, K., Case, J., & Brohl, K. (1998). *When Your Child Has Been Molested*. New York. Lexington Books.

Herman, J. (1997). *Trauma and Recovery*. New York. Basic Books.

Hunter, Mic. (1991). *Abused Boys*. New York. Fawcett Book Group.

Cavanaugh-Johnson, T. (1999). *Understanding Your Child's Sexual Behavior*. California. New Harbinger Publications.

Kristberg, W. (2000). *The Invisible Wound*. Nebraska. iUniverse, Inc.

Law, R. (1989). *Relapse Prevention with Sex Offenders*. New York. Guilford Press.

Ledray, L. (1995). Recovering from Rape. New York. Henry Holt & Co., Inc.

Levenson, J. & Morin, J. (2000). *Connections Workbook*. California. Sage Publications, Inc.

Maltz, W. & Arian, C. (2001). *The Sexual Healing Journey*. New York. Harper Trade.

Marshall, W., Anderson, D., & Fernandez, Y. (1999). *Cognitive Behavioral Therapy with Sex Offenders*. West Sussex, England. John Wiley & Son Ltd.

Miller, D. (1995). *Women Who Hurt Themsleves*. New York. Basic Book

Patterson, R. (2000). *The Assertiveness Workbook*. California. New Harbinger Publications.

Potter-Effron, R. & Potter-Effron, P. (1999). *Letting Go of Anger*. California. New Harbinger Publications.

Salter, A. (1999). *Treating Child Sex Offenders and Victims*. California. Sage Publications, Inc.

Salter, A. (1995). *Transforming Trauma*. California. Sage Publications, Inc.

Sommers-Flannagan, R., Sommers-Flannagan, J., & Elander, C. (2000). *Don't Divorce Us*. Virginia. American Counseling Association.

Steen, C. & Bear, E. (2000). *The Adult Relapse Prevention Workbook*. Vermont. Safer Society Press.

Stoppard, M. (1992). *The Magic of Sex*. New York. D K Publishing.

Whitfield, C. (1994). *Memory and Abuse*. Florida. Health Communications Inc.

Wiehe, V. (1995). *The Brother-Sister Hurt*. Vermont. Safer Society Press.

978-0-595-34804-6
0-595-34804-1